Praise for *Grab Life by*

Grab Life by the Dreams is no
lighthouse guiding you thro
seasoned travel guide, Karin shares the transformative power of
her personal journey using the EDIT method as her compass—
navigating through her own struggles, tackling the ever-persistent
inner critic, and proving that the road to reinvention is not a sprint
but a marathon.

~**Lucie Quigley**, Podcaster, Author, Midlife Mentor

Grab Life by the Dreams is a must-read for all women making a
change in their life. Each chapter helps to build a road map to
overcome the fear of change and take the steps to make it happen.
You will want to buy this for every woman in your life!

~**Dr. Cindy McGovern**, Bestselling Author of *Every Job Is a Sales Job* &
Sell Yourself

As someone who battled cancer and now works as a women's
leadership coach, I deeply resonate with this book. Karin openly
shares her journey of leaving corporate life to follow her heart,
while offering practical tools for reinvention. This motivating and
empowering read provides a confidence boost you didn't even
know you needed. Each chapter presents tangible exercises to
break free from feeling stuck. If you're a fan of self-help books,
don't miss *Grab Life by the Dreams*! It's relatable to every woman
and a must-read for those contemplating a life change. The workbook-style activities are priceless for overcoming challenges and
embracing new opportunities. If you're ready to break free from
the status quo, this book is an investment worth making.

~**Lucy Beato**, Author, Leadership & Business Coach

As the President of Women Confidence Builders, I am thrilled to endorse *Grab Life by the Dreams*. This book is a powerful and inspiring exploration of women and their careers, offering invaluable insights and guidance to help women unleash their true potential.

Grab Life by the Dreams serves as a beacon of empowerment for women at any stage of their careers. It offers practical advice, actionable strategies, and real-life examples of successful women who have overcome obstacles and pursued their dreams. Freeland's expertise and genuine passion for the subject shine through each page, making this book a must-read for anyone seeking inspiration and guidance in their professional journey.

What truly sets this book apart is its focus on fostering confidence in women. Freeland understands that confidence is the key ingredient for women to thrive in their careers, and she provides thought-provoking insights and practical exercises to help women build and maintain their self-assurance.

I wholeheartedly recommend *Grab Life by the Dreams* to all women who are seeking to make their mark in the professional world. Karin Freeland's profound understanding of the challenges and aspirations of women, combined with her empowering and uplifting writing style, makes this book an invaluable resource for personal and professional growth.

Prepare to be inspired, motivated, and equipped with the tools you need to overcome obstacles and achieve your dreams. *Grab Life by the Dreams* is a game-changer, and I am confident it will empower countless women to embrace their potential and create fulfilling careers.

~**Christi Powell**, President of Women Confidence Builders

In the ever-evolving journey of self-discovery and transformation, this book emerges as a beacon of clarity. The progression from challenging the status quo to fully owning one's power is crafted with profound wisdom and actionable insights. For anyone looking to transcend personal limitations and step into their fullest potential, this is your handbook. Dive in and embark on a transformative journey towards an empowered life!"

~**Amy Eliza Wong,** author of the critically acclaimed *Living On Purpose: Five Deliberate Choices to Realize Fulfillment and Joy*

In a world where many of us find ourselves feeling stuck and disconnected from our true dreams and passions, this book comes as a refreshing beacon of hope. Karin Freeland masterfully weaves together practical strategies with inspiring stories to guide readers on their journey toward their biggest goals.

~**Lori Oberbroeckling,** Best Selling Author and Productivity Coach

In *Grab Life by the Dreams*, Karin courageously shares how she made the leap from corporate to pursuing her dreams. She gives you easy-to-implement tools for the reinvention journey that so many desire to traverse.

~**Dame Clarissa Burt,** Founder/CEO of In the Limelight Media and Pluri-Award Winning International Best-Selling Author

Most women struggle to find their purpose and overcome imposter syndrome. If you can relate to this, then *Grab Life by the Dreams* is a must-read. It's the instant confidence boost you didn't know you needed. And it's written engagingly, so it's an easy read, as well as motivating and empowering!

~**Lisa Sweeney,** CEO of Business in Heels

Karin Freeland has done it once again with this wonderful book. *Grab Life by the Dreams* is a wonderful tale of aligned bravery, leading from golden, corporate handcuffs to living a life of dedication, service, and purpose.

The best part of this book is not the story, although it is wonderful; it is the actionable, grounded, and practical exercises for you to work through to make real, tangible, lasting change in your life. Having a formula to follow when making life changes gives a solid footing, creating greater ease and less fear when stepping into new territory. Karin delightfully guides you through how you can implement these structures in your own life as you build new habits, goals, and dreams.

Karin's trademark humour, love, and huge heart are evident in every word and light up the pages.

Do yourself a favour and add this to your "must gift" booklist for your friends.

~**Amanda Kate**, Self-Mastery Facilitator and Author of *Divine. Messy. Human. A Spiritual Guide to Prioritising Internal Truth over External Influence.*

Grab Life by the Dreams is not just a book—it's a transformative journey. Karin brilliantly bridges the gap between spirituality and practicality, leading readers on an empowering path from stagnation to purpose-driven action.

Chapter by chapter, you get clear, deep insights. What really hit home for me was the concept of changing how our brain is wired and the strong foundation of unwavering faith.

This book is a must-read for every woman determined not to settle. The workbook-style activities and invaluable 'Make it Happen' tips are worth their weight in gold!

Dive in and discover not just how to dream, but how to make those dreams your reality.

~**Maureen Chiana**, Neuroleadership & EQ Consultant, and Founder of The Mindsight Academy

GRAB LIFE

LIFE

by the

Dreams

GRAB
LIFE
by the
Dreams

THE ESSENTIAL GUIDE TO
GETTING UNSTUCK AND LIVING YOUR PURPOSE

KARIN FREELAND

Karin Freeland
Publishing

Published by Karin Freeland Publishing
Greenville, South Carolina

Karin Freeland
Publishing

Printed in the United States of America

Print ISBN: 979-8-9889598-0-9
eBook ISBN: 979-8-9889598-1-6

Library of Congress Control Number: 2023915937

Edited by Jessica Hatch, Hatch Editorial Services
Copyedited by Liz Crooks and Epstein Words
Proofread by Lucy Morton, LKM Editorial
Cover and Interior design by George Stevens, G Sharp Design, LLC
Back cover author photo by Yolanda Perez Photography LLC

You can connect with Karin on Instagram @karinfreeland and on Facebook at https://facebook.com/KarinFreelandLifeCoaching.

You can learn more about how Karin transforms women's lives at www.karinfreeland.com/life-coaching.

To God, Who knitted me together in my mother's womb and meant for me to be right here, right now.

ACKNOWLEDGMENTS

*To my family…*for entertaining my passions, patiently supporting my writing of another book, and loving me wholeheartedly. I know it's not always easy to endure, but I hope I inspire you to always follow your hearts and grab life by the dreams. Life is too short to live it any other way!

*To my editor, Jessica Hatch…*for helping me take my ideas and process and articulate them in such a digestible way. I'm forever grateful for your guidance and encouragement along the way. I know this book will impact even more lives because of your editing genius!

*To my clients…*for trusting me to help you write a new chapter in your life. I'm humbled to be your coach. I'm the lucky one who gets to work with such talented and powerful women. You inspire me to be better every day!

*To all the dreamers who feel stuck…*for inspiring me to write this book. I have been in your shoes and I know how dreadful it is. This is your moment to make a pivot and change your life forever. I can't wait to see how you EDIT Your Life™. I'll be cheering you on!

FOREWORD

Dear Dream Grabbers,

When I got the request on Instagram from a stranger to do a foreword to her book, I have to admit, I almost deleted the message without further exploration. While flattered, why would I add more work to my already crazy life? As a stress physiologist and keynote speaker I'm on the road a lot. To keep my wild schedule from getting out of hand saying "no" has become an artform. But my curiosity got the better of me. I love (as you'll read in this book) women with gumption – especially those set on helping other women find their own confidence and purpose. I owed Karin the courtesy of at least looking into her work before outright dismissing her request. After all, had I not made asks of dozens of other women who were strangers to me for my own purposes?

As I dove into *Grab Life by the Dreams: The Essential Guide to Getting Unstuck and Living Your Purpose*, I found myself impressed with its bias towards action. This book is not just a collection of words; it is a guiding light that illuminates the path towards embracing life's full potential and manifesting your dreams (in a way that even a hard-nosed scientist like me can appreciate!).

Far too often, we allow fear, doubt, and societal pressures to hold us captive in the clutches of stagnation. We forget that each one of us possesses the innate power to redefine our reality and live a life that aligns with our deepest aspirations (not just the things we fear the least). With this book, dear reader, you'll find your ability to reclaim your agency and unleash the potential that lies dormant within you—and Karin will be there with you every step of the way.

With her reassuring (and funny!) voice, stories from her personal life and professional clients, you'll discover invaluable insights and practical tools that will aid you in breaking free from the chains of inertia.

To grab life by the dreams is not merely an act of ambition; it is an embrace of action and authenticity. Consider this my own embrace of you, your journey, and your dreams.

Get to grabbing and stay fear(less)!

Dr. Rebecca Heiss
Fear(less)
www.rebeccaheiss.com
@drrebeccaheiss

TABLE OF CONTENTS

EDIT Your Life™

INTRODUCTION

Are you a dreamer? Do you feel like you're made for something more, a bigger purpose?

Good. Me too.

Do you desire to get unstuck and soothe that nagging voice in your soul telling you it's time for a change?

You're about to uncover the tools to help you do that.

Are you an action-taker determined to use the power and time you have here on Earth to make a more profound impact?

I can't wait to reveal the methodology to help you achieve that! But first, here's a glimpse at a defining moment in my reinvention journey, the journey that led me to launch and build a successful coaching business, write an award-winning memoir and now this book, and share my secret with you.

"Yes."

That one little word took me from defeated and on the brink of quitting my attempt at entrepreneurship to a deep belief in myself and my capabilities. It was the moment the Universe validated everything I had spent the past six months doing.

My first potential life coaching client had just become my first *paying* life coaching client. There were so many emotions swirling in my head and racing through my body after she said yes, but I knew I had to maintain my composure long enough to explain the payment process and the next steps for onboarding.

It's really happening! kept running through my mind. *I'm officially a life coach.* Of course, my website and certification already confirmed that, but this client was solid proof. My palms were sweating as I processed her credit card transaction. I was glad she was on Zoom and not sitting in the same room as me so I could mask my exhilaration.

After I got through explaining what would happen next for my client—don't you love the sound of that word? *Client*—and disconnected our call, I let out a huge victory whoop. I could barely form a sentence, I was so ecstatic. I leapt down the stairs two at a time, heading from my home office to the living room, where my kids and husband were waiting patiently on the couch for the verdict.

"She signed up!!" I screamed.

My family sprang from their seats and hugged me as we jumped up and down in a circle, my confused dog observing our frenzied celebration. It was the best $1,049 I had earned in years. (Yes, that was my initial rate. I had some confidence issues of my own to work through. Anyone who tells you they didn't when they started their business is probably lying.)

Seeing everyone share in my joy was heart-bursting in the best of ways. I had never seen my boys' eyes light up with pride for their mom's accomplishments before. They were finally old enough to understand how important this was for me, and they immediately began to share all the ways they thought I should spend my new income, not realizing what my cost of acquisition was. I listened intently, smiling so hard my cheeks hurt.

The first six months of my new life as a coach had been rocky. One second I was on a high, and the next I was as low as I could go. Being that I was a life coach, I felt like I had to be "on" 24/7 and maintain a bubbly, positive outlook, which was difficult to do, considering that everywhere I looked I saw (what I thought of as) more successful coaches claiming to earn seven figures, selling out online courses overnight, and making more than $10K a month. Meanwhile, I was struggling to get one single client!

My inner critic was loud and wanted to affirm everything she had told me in the past: *You can't leave corporate; you'll never make enough money. You don't even know how to run a business. Entrepreneurship isn't for people like you.* To say it felt like I was on a roller coaster is an understatement. Fortunately, I had a strong support network, which included an empowering coach of my own. She guided and challenged me to keep my mindset positive by focusing on what I could control. Further, I had a rock solid "why" that just wouldn't let me quit and a clear vision of what I wanted my life to look like. Even in my lowest, most self-doubting moments, I had known with certainty in my soul that I had the power to make it a reality. For once, I had bet on myself, and now that bet was paying dividends.

Why do I share this story with you? Two reasons. One: I want you to know that reinventing yourself isn't easy. Old habits often die hard. To reach that first yes, I had to work through months, if not years, of self-sabotage, negative self-talk, worrying about what others thought, and comparing myself to everyone around me. And two: I could have easily given up on my dreams in those early months, when everything was so uncertain. I could have gone back to the reliable if soul-crushing drudgery of my old corporate career, but then I wouldn't have been able to touch the dozens of lives of the women I've coached and the thousands of women this book will positively impact.

Reinvention doesn't happen overnight. Don't let anyone tell you it does. It's a steady process that takes a different amount of time for everyone. It depends on so many factors, like your mindset, your upbringing, your financial situation and disposable income, how big your dream is, how averse you are to risk, your level of confidence in your abilities to achieve it, your support system, how badly you want it, and so many other things. But don't let any of this deter you; it can all be overcome.

As you read this book, the only person I want you to compare yourself to is the you of yesterday. And by yesterday, I don't mean literally the day before today. I've had my fair share of bum days, so if, in my six-month roller coaster period of daily highs and lows, I had looked at myself the previous day, when I was quite literally doing better, that would have been a major deterrent to my forward momentum. Instead, I looked at the me of the week before, the month before, the year before. Was I better than that version of Karin? Yes? Then I needed to keep going.

A well-known African proverb states, "If you want to go fast, go alone; if you want to go far, go together." Do you know when I really started to see movement in my life, in the direction of my dreams? When I got a coach of my own. When I asked for help. When I realized I simply couldn't get to a life I loved all by myself.

If you're anything like me, then I know right now you're cringing at the idea of asking for help or publicly admitting you need support, so here's your first lesson: *there is nothing wrong with requesting help.* It's not a sign of weakness. Quite the opposite: it's a sign of strength and courage, a key ingredient to your success formula—the strength to admit when you need support and the courage to follow through on what that guide is teaching you. If you read that and thought, *Well, I've got a long way to go*, take heart. Consider me a guide, and consider the fact that you picked up this book as a means of self-*help* (i.e., support). The fact that you've started reading this book is a sign you have the necessary strength and courage within you.

There is so much to be learned from others who have been there and done that. That's why my coaching clients choose to work with me. They know I've already walked through the fire and come out on the other side better for it. In the years since I snagged my first coaching client, I've:

- won a Readers' Favorite award for my memoir, which helps women laugh as they learn to love their bodies;
- raised over $2,000 to fight period poverty through my work with the Alliance for Period Supplies;
- been a guest on more than sixty-five podcasts, inspiring others to get unstuck and balance their priorities;
- and coached dozens of women to reach their professional and personal goals and reinvent their lives.

While the lessons I'm teaching in this book are supported by proven studies run by a cohort of professional psychologists and businesspeople, every one of them is based on real-life experiences, ones my coaching clients and I have lived through, with practical applications and exercises for you to complete.

You might be wondering, *Can a book really change my life?* To which I would respond, "Hell yes!" I had my own experience with a life-altering book in 2017 when I read Helene Lerner's *In Her Power*. What I had been doing wasn't working for my life, and, thanks to Helene, I was finally in a place where I could accept that something had to give. She wrote in a way that felt as if she knew exactly what I was going through, and she shared concrete strategies for how to tap into my power and change my circumstances. My hope is that you are ready to receive the messages in this book. If you are, you will truly experience a transformation.

So, what can you expect next? Part 1 of *Grab Life by the Dreams* will help you discover how you can be more in tune with the dreams you have for your life and how you can walk through change with a firm and fearless commitment. Part 2 will share specific steps you can take to help you reach your fulfillment, such as turning inward, shifting your mindset, and exploring your spirituality. Part 3 will share my specific process to EDIT Your Life™. Because this process has been used successfully by me and my clients for the past three years, I've included client examples along the way to demonstrate how these steps applied in other women's lives too. If we can do it, so can you.

I recommend reading this book in order, from start to finish. While you could jump around among the sections, you may find it harder to apply my principles if you haven't built a firm foundation around them in previous chapters.

Beyond inviting you to continue reading from cover to cover, I want to also, more importantly, encourage you to start taking action. To this end, I've provided a bonus "Make It Happen" section at the end of each chapter. Do. The. Work. A Harvard study published in 2019 demonstrated that students scored higher on tests when they practically applied a lesson rather than just sitting through a lecture. If you merely read this book, sure, you'll see some surface-level benefit. But if you want to experience transformation—real, tangible, lasting differences in your life—you must implement everything you learn. Do the exercises full-out. Ask yourself the tough questions. Journal your deepest feelings. If you play full-out, you'll reap more benefits than I can count. The ripple effect of your newfound self will be too great to articulate.

And whatever you do, don't quit! You never know how you will impact the world!

Now, go grab *your* life by the dreams.

Karin

Part 1
Busting the Status Quo

Chapter 1

Your "Oh Shit!" Moment

See, what you're meant to do when you have
a mid-life crisis is buy a fast car, aren't you? Well,
I've always had fast cars. It's not that. It's the fear
that you're past your best. It's the fear that the stuff
you've done in your past is your best work.

—ROBBIE COLTRANE

2:43 a.m.

I peered over my husband's shoulder at the clock. I could barely see the time. The three glasses of wine I'd chugged before bed were coming back to bite me, as they did every night.

"Ugh." I sighed faintly as I rolled myself out of bed and shuffled around the frame of our queen-size bed that barely fit in our dormered Cape. I was careful not to drill my shin into the corner post as I had done so many other nights.

Entering the bathroom, I pressed the lowest setting on our dimmer switch. There was just enough light to make out the toilet. Lifting the lid, I turned myself around and sat down. As I sat there, elbows on knees and chin resting in hands, my mind drifted.

> *Isn't it crazy that I've been sleeping and have no recollection of it? The world keeps turning, but I'm completely unaware of what's happening. I wonder if that's what it's like when we die.*
>
> *Total darkness and nothingness. Huh.*

That's when it hit me. Actually, it had been hitting me for months.

> *Oh my God. I'm going to die one day! How do I make it stop? Do I eat better? Exercise more? It's hopeless—this is the one thing I can't control. Why can't I live forever? How can the world just keep going on without me? What about my kids? I don't want to die!!*

The wave of terror began without warning and moved swiftly throughout my body. A feeling of weightlessness as if I were floating in space consumed me momentarily. The total darkness I had imagined felt real. My cheeks were searing hot as tears erupted from my eyes, streaming across them. My voice, though? Totally silent. I didn't want to make a peep for fear my husband would wake up and see the headcase that sat on our toilet: me!

I thrust my hands over my eyes, wiping away the tears. I'd already let several fall onto my lap. Grabbing toilet paper, I took care of business and flushed, taking that one opportunity to sniffle fiercely, knowing the sound would be masked. I then stared myself down in the dark mirror.

Get your shit together, Karin. Danny is going to walk in here and think you've lost your damn mind. Everyone dies. You're not even going to know it happened, so what are you so freaked out about? Stop doing this. Stop thinking about this every night.

With one final, shaky inhale, I resolved to push all these feelings out of my mind and back into the depths from which they had surged. I'd be lucky if I could get another two and a half hours of sleep at this point. I didn't want puffy eyes in the morning; it might signal to my family or coworkers that something was wrong.

I'm a big girl. I can handle my problems on my own.

I exited the bathroom, gingerly sliding into bed so as not to wake my husband. A few snores from him were all the reassurance I needed that he was none the wiser. The only problem now was that I couldn't escape the nightmare. The one inescapable fact that had haunted me since the deaths of my great-uncle and great-aunt just six and two months earlier: someday, unbeknownst to me, I was going to die.

That thought scared the shit out of me.

Sometimes it takes an earth-shattering, catastrophic event, like two deaths in the span of four months, or a major health scare like a cancer diagnosis, to wake you up. Other times, it's a slow and quiet build, like a pot coming to a boil that suddenly pops the lid off. While the process that gets us to this state varies, the outcome is the same. I call this the "Oh Shit!" Moment. It's probably self-explanatory, but here I go anyway. It's that moment that you realize your time here is finite; that, like a carton of milk, you are going to expire. Kaput. Be no more. Hasta luego. Sayonara. Game over. Stick a fork in me, I'm done. You get the picture. It's the moment you're staring your mortality in the face—or perhaps the Grim Reaper.

For me, it was all just a bit too much to take in. If you've had your own "Oh Shit!" Moment, you'll likely agree. Religion and spirituality—which we'll discuss in Chapter 6—aside, there is something incredibly terrifying about not knowing what happens after we leave this earthly existence. Thoughts about it can become all-consuming, gripping you day and night at the most inconvenient times. Once you've had the moment, there's no going back.

In all honesty, I had a lot to be thankful for. A lot of other people would've killed to be in my position. I had a good marriage; my husband and I were a team and were faithful to each other. I had two healthy boys who were relatively well-behaved. We had plenty of money to live an amazing lifestyle and enjoy ourselves (when I wasn't working). I had a roof over my head, even though my kitchen was tiny and I couldn't open my dishwasher and refrigerator at the same time. I had a Benz in the driveway. A fancy title at work. And so much more. I don't want to seem ungrateful. It was just that something very important was missing: FULFILLMENT. I'm sharing this with you because I know a lot of high achievers feel the same. However, not wanting to seem ungrateful is not reason enough to stay in an unfulfilling situation.

Fulfillment, for our purposes, is defined as deep satisfaction or happiness realized as a result of achieving your full potential or purpose. Clearly there is no one-size-fits-all object or experience that can be labeled as fulfillment. It's different for each of us because we are all designed for a different purpose. Are you experiencing feelings of unfulfillment? If so, permission granted to admit it.

Turns out the things that society promises will bring you fulfillment don't always pan out. All the money and titles I'd earned at work didn't fill the gaping hole in my soul. All the purses and designer clothes felt empty and useless. All the wine in the world couldn't cure my pain. Why? Because there is another piece to the fulfillment puzzle: how we are motivated.

The things that motivate us fall into two basic categories: extrinsic motivation and intrinsic motivation. *Extrinsic motivation* occurs when we complete a task because we know we will get an external reward or recognition for completing it—or because we feel that we will let others down if we don't. I was going to work every day and doing my job to get a bigger title and paycheck. Extrinsic motivation. I was no longer enjoying my job, but it was what I had done for so long that it seemed silly to question it.

Meanwhile, *intrinsic motivation* is any situation in which a task is done for the simple gratification of doing the task itself. It's being inspired to take an action for the pure love of doing it. Unlike my life before my "Oh Shit!" Moment, I now wake up and get to coach amazing women every day so they experience more fulfillment and avoid the pain I went through. That's a lot more motivating for me.

Think about it. How are you motivated? Maybe that's changed over time or depending on the area of your life we're talking about? I was very motivated and fulfilled by my job in the early years. I loved me some external validation, and it motivated a lot of my decisions. As I got older, though, that waned. I no longer cared about the fancy titles or large paychecks. I needed something deeper, more meaningful. I longed to tap into my intrinsic motivation, although I didn't understand that at the time.

On a similar note, I have friends who love being a mom. Motherhood fulfills them on an intrinsic level. And, yes, I love being a mom, too, but I found, around the time of my 3 a.m. crying jags, that motherhood alone didn't fulfill me—and that's okay! I wasn't defective, and if you relate to this, neither are you. I have friends who are fulfilled by their nine-to-five jobs. Ultimately, I wasn't. Again, that's okay. I'm normal, and so are you. I have friends who are fulfilled by volunteering their time, donating large sums of money, or rescuing animals. The key is that whatever you're doing, it should be because it brings you happiness and fulfillment, an inner sense of accomplishment.

But as I had these realizations, I still wasn't able to make a change. I lacked empowerment. I was sad all the time. Stressed to the point of grinding my teeth in my sleep and needing a root canal and night guard. I was restless in my marriage. I wanted passion, like the old days. Instead, it felt like I had a hot roommate without any of the benefits. Every day was the same mundane routine. We had a list of things that had to be done every night, and we'd check them off as we went: make kids' lunches, give dog water, run dishwasher, make coffee, on and on. While it kept us organized, I grew to resent that list. It felt as hopeless as Bill Murray waking up to "I Got You, Babe" every morning for thousands of mornings in *Groundhog Day*. Parenthood was exhausting and not at all what I had imagined. (No one told me asking your kid to brush their teeth 273 times a morning was normal!)

Most people had no idea I felt this way because I was skilled at faking happiness. Like a lot of women, I knew how to play the game and what to say to hide my pain. I thrived at dancing on the edge of burnout, wearing my workaholism like a badge of honor. The busier I was, the more valuable I must be, right? I tuned out all nudges from my heart and turned up the volume in my head.

*Keep going. You can handle this. Stop dreaming about
a different life.*

If this resonates with you, you're not alone. Most of us shut
out the desires of our heart by listening to the practicali-
ties of our head. I was the breadwinner for my family. How
could I possibly walk away from my job? Not to mention the
question of worthiness. Did I really feel capable and worthy
of a better life? The jury was out for a bit longer. The burning
question remained: What impact am I really having on the
world? No matter how hard I tried to stretch my marketing
job's value, it felt like it didn't exist.

My husband, on the other hand, recited his life mission
to me one night, and while it was absolutely beautiful—to
raise our boys to be upstanding and productive members of
society—I felt even more frustrated than before. What's *my*
mission? What was I put here to do? What's my purpose? As
I contemplated these questions, I became acutely aware of one
thing: I was stuck! I came up empty at every turn.

Part of the problem was I had no blueprint on how
I could get from here—stuck and hopeless—to there—happy
and fulfilled.

This might sound like it's all bad news, but that's not the
case. Let me offer a little glimmer of hope for you.

The beauty of having your "Oh Shit!" Moment is that you
get more time to enjoy your second chance. I'm thankful I had
mine at thirty-nine years old, but please don't misunderstand
me. If you're coming to these questions a little older or have

never had them before you picked up this book, it's not too late. It's never too late for a reinvention! This book is still very much for you. As long as you're breathing, you have an opportunity to change course and create the life you were meant to live.

Whether you've had your "Oh Shit!" Moment or not, now is the time to do one very important step: honestly acknowledge what's not working in your life. I know you've heard the little voices telling you where you're unhappy. Listen to them. Confront them. Own them. Without this step, you'll stay stuck on the mundane hamster wheel of everyday life. And that's no way to live at all! I want more for you. I want you to be able to say with 100 percent certainty what's working and what's not working in your life. You may be tempted to think you don't know or may even be embarrassed to acknowledge it. I'm inviting you to be brave.

Let's use my situation in 2019 as an example.

What Wasn't Working:

- My job
- My commute
- Lack of friendships and sense of community
- Distance from family
- Real intimacy with my husband
- Quality time with my kids—chauffeuring them to and from sports didn't count

These were some pretty major aspects of my life I was struggling with. Some had become unfulfilling over time, like my job. Others were casualties of my success, like my lack of friendships and intimacy. The thing is, I stopped my list right there. What a mistake! I could have told you, and anyone else who would listen to me vent, all the things that were wrong with my life.

What I couldn't tell others, myself included, was what *was* working. I never bothered to take inventory of all the things that were going well. Herein lay the rest of the problem. Anyone can complain. There is very little empowerment required for that. I couldn't tell people what was working because I didn't know what I actually wanted out of life. I had nothing to compare my life to, no North Star I was tracking toward. While venting to a coworker one day, he asked me point-blank, "What would you regret not doing before you died?" I stumbled over my words, trying to articulate some semblance of an answer. The truth was, I didn't know. I felt like I had just been caught naked in public.

> *Wow. How is it I can clearly identify things I don't like,*
> *but I haven't the foggiest clue about what I do want?*
> *I should know that, right?*

That thought struck me deep down in my soul and motivated me (intrinsically, I might add!) to find out. I knew my list of regrets would be long if I kept going on my current course, but what would those regrets be, and how could I rectify this before things got any further out of hand?

In hindsight, it's easy to see why I couldn't articulate those things at that moment. I'd been running 100 miles an hour since I was born. Well, maybe not from birth but certainly from high school. I started my first job at fourteen, danced competitively, maintained respectable grades, and had a hyperactive social calendar. I was the queen of fear of missing out before it was ever called FOMO. In college, I worked all four years, was active in my sorority, studied abroad, and even took twenty-four credits my senior year so I could graduate with a double major. After college, I hustled as a waitress while pursuing my acting dreams. I ran from audition to photo shoot to work all day, every day, cramming in as much as I could, sleeping as little as humanly necessary. Later in life, my work ethic would only intensify, as I worked full time while raising two boys, trying to maintain a marriage, writing a book, and starting not one but two businesses.

I literally had never taken a pause in my life. Perhaps you're nodding along because this sounds familiar. I know type A, driven personalities will relate. So, now is your chance to take a pause and reflect.

Experiencing my own "Oh Shit!" Moment, catalyzed by the death of my family members, helped me gain perspective on what's important to me. Their passing, while sad, gave birth to my new, purpose-driven life. A life that now touches so many others. I'll share more about how this unfolded and how I synthesized it into the repeatable steps anyone can follow in the coming chapters. But first…

I want to create an opportunity for you to have a contained "Oh Shit!" Moment. Now, I certainly don't want you to experience a loved one's death or some wild existential crisis. That's not what I'm saying. Rather, I'm urging you to start examining your life by contemplating this thought over your morning coffee now so you're not weeping on a toilet at three in the morning later. You have an opportunity to turn things around right now, but you have to actually do something about it. I say that firmly because even if everyone eventually confronts their mortality, not everyone does something about it. It's true that the pages of this book may unearth some hidden truths for you, and that can be uncomfortable, to say the least. But to ignore that would be a travesty! Can you imagine being given a second chance at life and not taking it? Completely disregarding the Universe and staying on the status quo course? Such a shame. But that's not you. You're an action taker!

With action comes change. I know change can feel scary, but I'll help you overcome your fears throughout this book. Change is also incredibly beautiful and fulfilling. Right now, imagine you are a caterpillar. You're not bad-looking—a little hairy, but it could be worse. You're about to make a cocoon and undergo a metamorphosis. When you come out on the other side of this book, if you've done the work, you will be a beautiful butterfly, shedding your old skin for something that suits you better. You are not throwing out your soul. The inside, the core that is you, will still be you—just more authentic and happier, because you're showing up on the outside the way you feel on the inside.

How do I know this? Because I was once the caterpillar, too, and now I'm the butterfly. Unfortunately, I was in my cocoon for four long, tumultuous years. But you don't have to ride the struggle bus that long because you have me, your Life Reinvention Coach. I'm going to be here with you every step of the way, guiding you on this journey and giving you practical exercises to help you build the life you want—dare I say, the life you've always dreamed of having.

Now, don't let the word *reinvention* scare you. While the dictionary definition is "the action or process through which something is changed so much that it appears to be entirely new," it doesn't always mean drastic changes. Sometimes, the smallest internal tweaks to your life can have the biggest impact, like looking at a situation with a positive mindset or strengthening your confidence. But if you're down to blow up entire areas of your life and come out on the other side completely revamped, that's great! I've got your back too. It's really up to you how much you reinvent and how fast. (You can breathe a sigh of relief now.)

I'm grateful you bought this book, and I know reading it will absolutely provide you with immense value. If you want transformation, though, you *have* to put in the hard work every step of the way.

No procrastination. No excuses.

Promise? Good. Let's get started.

Make It Happen

For our first "Make It Happen" section, I've picked three exercises that benefited me right at the beginning of my journey, right after I decided to do something about those 3 a.m. "Oh Shit!" Moments.

Journaling

Let's start with some journaling. It's one of my favorite activities because it helps you bring your subconscious to the surface. It helps you stare your thoughts in the face and really question if you believe what you've written. We are going to dig up those feelings you've intentionally been hiding. (Trust me. You'll thank me later.)

First, ask yourself the following questions. Note: do *not* self-edit. I know there will be a temptation to leave certain feelings out or avoid painful areas. Instead, lean in and go there. That's where the magic and transformation happen. There is no need to censor yourself.

- What's *not* working in my life?

- What *is* working in my life?

◦ What's my biggest pain point? The thing that, if I changed it tomorrow, the majority of my agony would go away?

◦ What could my life mission be? (Don't worry if you don't know for certain. I didn't either at first. Just start playing with some ideas and seeing how you react to them.)

For the next few days, reread what you wrote. Go to a quiet place and read your answers out loud. See how it feels to hear yourself say your thoughts. Do you believe them? Are they still valid? There's no point in upsetting something that's working, but don't mistake this for not changing something that is preventing you from reaching a goal. For instance, let's say you're making great money at your job, but you're unhappy. In this case, the money is working, but the job is not. It could be worth upsetting the money in exchange for your mental health.

Notice where your heart is excited and where your head tries to talk you out of things. And vice versa—where is your head leading you, and why is your heart lagging? The more clarity you can get on the answers to these questions, the better you'll be able to tackle the next steps.

Happy journaling!

Practicing Gratitude

It's a lot easier to change your outlook than your circumstances. Sometimes it's the only thing you actually have control over. An easy place to start is with gratitude. According to *Positive Psychology*, "The effects of gratitude, when practiced daily, can be almost the same as medications. It produces a feeling of long-lasting happiness and contentment, the physiological basis of which lies at the neurotransmitter level." Without getting all scientific on you, it basically changes your brain's wiring. The more you practice gratitude, the stronger the connection in your brain, and the faster you truly feel grateful and content with your life. Further, it triggers dopamine and serotonin, two neurochemicals needed to lift your mood. Think about it like your happy juice: one part gratitude, one part dopamine, and one part serotonin equals loving life.

Depending on where you are in your journey, it may seem like there isn't much to be grateful for, but research has shown gratitude is life's natural antidepressant. One of my clients started working with me shortly after her mom passed away. If there was ever a time for a coach, it was at that moment, and the Universe had lined that up perfectly. I knew she was experiencing tremendous heartbreak and wanted to see if this exercise, Gratitude Garden, would help. I explained the exercise, set my timer for two minutes, and away she went...and went...and went. Two minutes hit and she was still naming things! The woman who had just lost her mom had no problem naming two minutes' worth of things to be grateful for. Three minutes, four minutes... finally at five minutes I stopped her. She had an expression of deep relief and peace on her face. We both smiled, knowing everything was going to be all right. If she could find something to be grateful for at such a difficult time, I know you can too.

I call this exercise Gratitude Garden because we are planting the seeds of gratitude in our hearts.

- Start by going to a quiet place (e.g., your bedroom, your car, your closet, a secluded pond or nature trail, the bathroom, a conference room at work).

- Set a timer on your phone for two minutes. I like this amount of time because it forces you to get beyond the surface-level stuff that everyone says and get to the meat. It's also not so short that it doesn't have the full impact or so long that you can't fit it into your schedule.

- Start saying or writing out *all* the things you're grateful for.

Don't stop until the timer goes off. If you're really on a roll, feel free to keep going beyond the two minutes.

Most of you will get a solid minute in and then start struggling. I encourage you to not overthink this. It can be as big as, "Thank you for my spouse," or as mundane as, "Thank you for peanut butter and jelly sandwiches so I don't have to cook tonight."

The point is you're exploring another way to look at all the good in your life and the things that are working just fine. Any time you need a little pick-me-up, you can come back to this exercise and remind yourself of all you have to be grateful for already.

Sitting in Silence

For some, this might actually be the hardest activity. Giving yourself time to be alone with your thoughts and energy is key to understanding your deepest desires. Start with ten minutes—you can increase it over time. I call this activity Sitting in Silence, but you can also lie down. (On your back on a yoga mat can be a comforting position.) Feel free to set a timer if it helps you focus.

As you sit in silence, allow your thoughts to wander. Release any judgment as it comes up. Forgive yourself and others as needed. Dream freely. Notice repeating thoughts or patterns.

I recommend keeping a journal or piece of paper close by so you can take notes if something big pops into your brain. Pause your timer to capture the thought. Then, after you've taken down the note, resume your timer and go back to your silence.

Chapter 2

Hello. This Is the Universe Calling!

When you begin to dance with the energy of the Universe your life flows naturally, incredible synchronicity presents itself, creative solutions abound and you experience freedom.

—GABBY BERNSTEIN, *THE UNIVERSE HAS YOUR BACK: HOW TO FEEL SAFE AND TRUST YOUR LIFE NO MATTER WHAT*

Have you ever experienced a bittersweet mix of emotions, like joy for others and sadness for yourself at the same time? You might even be excited to be a participant in the other person's joy, such as attending a dinner celebrating a friend's promotion when you hate your job or attending a cousin's wedding when you're perennially single, and yet the other more negative emotion remains.

Though this emotional mixture tends to sting, I have come to find it interesting when it happens to me. If you're listening carefully to the Universe, I've found the emotional sting often comes right before it sends you a sign.

In 2017, two years before my panic attacks and "Oh Shit!" Moments peaked, while working for a Fortune 500 telecommunications company, I was sent to Las Vegas for a trade show.

At this point, corporate life had burned me out. I'd had the carrot pulled away from me one too many times. After a year of being chief of staff to the president of the wireline division, my position ended abruptly when he announced his retirement. The role of marketing director I had been promised was nowhere in sight, and I was dumped back into middle management. Every day was a constant reminder that I wasn't valued as much as I had thought. As usual—at that time in my life, anyway—I masked the pain with copious amounts of alcohol. Deep down I knew I wanted to be anywhere but Vegas, working for anyone but this company, doing anything but what I was doing; however, I had a job to do, and I was innately driven to make sure it was done well.

On the second day of the expo, I begged off from a customer appreciation happy hour at an ice bar and dashed back to my hotel room. I'd seen a magazine ad for a show my first night in our hotel, and I wanted to give it another look.

Once safely in my hotel room with the door locked, I kicked off my heels and spread the magazine out flat on the king-size bed. Flipping pages frantically, I finally found exactly what I was looking for: The Jabbawockeez. One of my favorite hip-hop dance crews was performing at the MGM Grand. I knew in my gut I had to attend, so I shrugged off my insecurities about going alone and called for ticket prices. The woman on the phone assured me the aisle seat she picked for me was a good one, and I shelled out a little over a hundred dollars for it.

Later that evening I sat in the dark theater, waiting in anticipation for the curtains to open and the dancing to commence. It had been so many years since I had danced or been onstage, so not only excitement but also a deep sadness settled into my body. It took a moment to realize what I was feeling. I was grieving my dreams while I sat in the audience, about to watch someone else live theirs. It was similar to how I had felt after college, being a background actress on *All My Children*, *Guiding Light*, and *As the World Turns*. Heck, it was how I felt being stuck in middle management while others less capable than I was were promoted to directorships. I longed to be the one in the spotlight, so it hurt to see others succeeding even though I was genuinely happy for them. There was a tinge of jealousy, seeing how the Jabbawockeez had followed their dreams while acknowledging I had given up on mine.

As the spotlight flicked on and the dancers took the stage, though, my emotions quickly shifted. I sat in awe and admiration, watching them grace the room with their talent. There was a lot of audience participation throughout the show. Like a giddy schoolgirl at a junior high dance, I kept hoping they'd pick me to come onstage, but they never did.

In a rare move, I stood up and danced in the aisle, all by myself. Feeling freer than I'd felt in years, I didn't care who was looking at me. I was shedding the restraints of my corporate persona. I was fully present in the moment. I couldn't *not* dance.

The final routine was performed to Kid Cudi's "Pursuit of Happiness (Nightmare)." In it, the Jabbawockeez portrayed the way so many people trundle through life like zombies, going through the motions, one day at a time, half dead. It was like a knife right to my heart.

That's me, I thought. *I'm the zombie! I'm the one who has lost all her dreams. I'm half dead, drowning in a bed of sorrow. But how do I wake up? Help! Me, in row 5, can you help me?*

Of course, no one could. At least, no one I could physically see in the theater. As the show came to an end and I hailed a cab to go back to my hotel room, emotions flooded into me again, but I sent them packing and refocused on work. That MO had served me well in the past; why not employ it again now?

The rest of the Vegas trip was filled with boring trade show duties, and before I knew it, I was back in Jersey, where I lived at the time, and resuming the daily zombie grind. But something had stirred in me. I couldn't shake that song from my head. Was it a sign? Was someone trying to tell me something? Was I made for more? Destined for a different path? Or was I falling into the woo-woo that I had rejected so vehemently in the past?

I'd never been one for the woo-woo.

What's the woo-woo? you may be wondering. It's an umbrella term for all the mystical stuff; the supernatural; the think-it-and-it-will-happen mentality; tarot cards telling your future; astrology; quantum leaps; and unconventional ideas that just don't seem like they have any scientific or practical basis to them.

It might sound like something solely meant for New Age shops with beaded curtains and scarves over the lamps, but you see it all the time at business conferences. The speaker asks everyone to stand up and close their eyes and envision their wildest dreams coming true. Before my Vegas trip, I would have one eye open, wondering who would be crazy enough— or stupid enough—to do this. I got the same feeling whenever there was excessive, cult-like cheerleading at work. A trophy that our company was awarded was once passed around at a town hall meeting, and some employees actually kissed it. They kissed a plastic JD Powers award.

But maybe, just maybe, I was being a little too closed-minded? Maybe the Universe really was sending me signs? Maybe the subtle nudges were calling to me? Maybe the coincidences I experienced were something more—a synchronicity?

Fortunately, the Universe is patient, gently prodding us time and time again until we can no longer ignore its attempted interventions. The final straw that allowed me to give in to this concept of signs was during my "Oh Shit!" Moment days, when I was told about the movie *The Secret*. I'd heard about Rhonda Byrne's book years earlier on *Oprah* but had never bothered to dig any deeper than what was shared on the show.

Could watching this movie really change my life? Turns out, the answer was yes! It was like that ancient proverb: when the student is ready, the teacher will appear. *The Secret* was my teacher, and I was finally ready to receive its message, as evidenced by the epic mindset shift I experienced while watching the movie. Its explanation of the *Law of Attraction*—a belief that positive thoughts bring positive results into a person's life while negative thoughts bring negative ones— was exactly what I needed to see and hear at that precise moment. I found that I gelled with its foundational concept, that thoughts are a form of energy and that positive energy attracts success in all areas of one's life.

Some of you may also have heard the term *manifesting* before, which is similar but slightly different. Manifesting is a process that involves intentionally creating or bringing about specific outcomes or desires in one's life. It often involves setting clear intentions, visualizing desired outcomes, and taking inspired action toward those goals.

Call it what you will; the Universe had smacked me over the head, and now it all clicked: *I have the power to change my destiny and call in the positive things I seek in my life.* I learned that reputable thought leaders like Jack Canfield, Marci Shimoff, and Marie Diamond had all had the Law of Attraction play out in their lives. If it could work for them, why not me? There was nowhere to go but up from my rock bottom, so why not give it a shot? According to all of these successful people, the Universe was going to give me whatever I desired based on my thoughts and actions.

You might be asking yourself, Why would the Universe, or your Higher Power, take the time to reach out and send you signs? Are we really worthy of this level of communication? Absolutely you are. You—yes, you, reading this book!—were designed for a unique and important purpose. Your creation was not by accident. You are here on Earth at this specific time for a reason. Therefore, the Universe is always interested in guiding you in achieving that purpose—the purpose you were destined to fulfill. When we live out our purpose, we are contributing to the world and having a more meaningful impact on it. Not only is this good for those who benefit from your purpose and for yourself; this is also how you reach ultimate fulfillment in all areas of your life—career, health, relationships, and even finances—because you are in alignment with what you were created to do.

As I started to implement a practice of positive thoughts and of listening to my feelings more, I could no longer ignore the biggest sign that I was being sent: I was not meant for corporate life any longer. The Universe had been trying to tell me this since 2017—even before then, if I'm honest—but

I hadn't been listening because I wasn't willing (yet) to put the signs into action.

If you take anything away from my early experiences of listening to the Universe, I hope it's that you need to be ready to receive its messages and be willing to surrender to them. You may not be sure about some of the messages you receive. You may see them as inconveniences or frustrations. You might not even like them at first! But allow yourself to sit with them. Write them down so you can reflect on them further.

Perhaps you're receiving a message that reduces your financial position in the short term, but that will increase it tenfold in the long run. That can be scary to hear, and you may be hesitant to follow through, but remember the emotional mix that happened to me as I watched the Jabba-wockeez perform? This is where you'll need to let go of your way and trust the way of the Universe. If you aren't willing to surrender, reaching your ultimate potential will be difficult. But don't panic. As I stated before, the Universe is patient and will never give up on trying to reach you.

In addition to messages about your finances, you might receive signs in a plethora of areas, such as:

- Relationships – Whom you should be connected to platonically or in business, or a romantic relationship you should pursue
- Career – The jobs you are meant to do and the impact you're meant to have on others

ᴐ⊘ Finances – The money you're meant to receive or share with others

ᴐ⊘ Health – The steps you need to take to get healthier or the risks you should avoid

We're about to discuss a couple of ways the Universe may send you signs, but before we do, please note: while I'm inviting you to be open-minded and explore potential signs, I am not suggesting you should do anything outside of your values. Some of you may be uncomfortable with certain practices, like Reiki healing or tarot cards. I know women who don't even like essential oils because they feel taboo. Perhaps your practice would involve a more targeted prayer life or opening a page of the Bible and randomly selecting a passage to see what sign that reading is sending you. It's important to know your boundaries and stay true to yourself while seeking guidance in your life. As we go through the rest of the chapter, do what makes you most comfortable and jettison the rest.

Through Synchronicity

One way the Universe might call to you is through synchronicity. *Synchronicity* is the idea that events in your life can be related in meaning or in purpose, without actually being linked by cause and effect. Basically, they appear related, you can't explain how, yet they have a specific significance to you. For example, what are the chances that the Jabbawockeez would have a show called JREAMZ, during which they would perform to that Kid Cudi song, at the same time I got sent to Vegas, happened to see the ad, and got lucky enough to be relieved from the ice bar experience? Not likely.

Of course, now I can see that the Universe was telling me to leave the corporate world. So why didn't I immediately act on it? At the time, it was an inconvenient truth. I didn't actually know how to act on it; even if I had known, I wasn't empowered enough then to follow through. It was a seed planted nevertheless, and that in and of itself was valuable. As the signs stacked up over the coming years, it became a sign that was no longer avoidable.

When you get a synchronous message like this, the question now becomes: What is the Universe trying to tell me? What signs could I be missing in my life? Whether you believe in God, a Higher Power, or something else, we all experience signs, whether we realize it or not. How? It could be a song on the radio at the right time, a person you meet, a job you don't get, money that lands in your lap unexpectedly, a dream about someone you haven't seen in years, a sermon at church, a billboard you drive by about a company that's hiring, a number that appears repeatedly, a friendship that ends, or anything else for which you can identify meaning and connection to your life. The list is endless because everyone's signs are different depending on their circumstances.

Through Silver Linings

For example, when I was working for an energy company, it seemed like nothing I did was good enough. Sales was brutal, always tearing down the marketing department's ideas and thinking I wasn't doing enough to support local initiatives; meanwhile, HQ thought I wasn't doing enough to support their global initiatives. It felt like being sandwiched between a rock and hard place. I'd finally had it and decided to apply to a job with another energy company. I was a shoo-in for the role. I had the credentials, the background, and some innovative ideas that would increase the company's market share. I also knew that, based on the size of the role and the longer commute, my hours would increase. No doubt that would include more stress I didn't need, given that I had recently been diagnosed with silent acid reflux. (Ladies, listen to your bodies!)

Spoiler alert: I didn't get the job. I was so angry and frustrated. I sulked and consoled myself with a bottle of wine or three. *Why hadn't I been selected? What did I do wrong? Was I doomed to stay in my current soul-sucking job forever? Maybe I just wasn't cut out for corporate anymore?* I wrote all of these things and more in my journal.

Looking back, I realize it wasn't something I did wrong. The Universe just had other plans for me—better plans. My Higher Power knew that if I got a new job with more money and a better title, I'd seal the coffin a little tighter on my dreams. I'd constrict myself even further than I already had. I had to *lose* that job to *win* my new life, the life I couldn't yet see clearly, but which was already in the works.

What about you? Could there be a silver lining to some of the negative things that have happened in your life? Perhaps when the sale fell through for that dream house, it opened up a door to get a house in a better part of town with better schools. Or maybe in fifth grade, when your band teacher assigned you to the trumpet instead of the saxophone, you realized you had a knack for that instrument and eventually earned a music scholarship for college. This isn't just about little things either, or about what we've come to socially refer to as "First World problems." For instance, losing a child can be devastating, and yet so many grieving parents choose to donate their children's organs to save the lives of other children, creating a silver lining.

Through People in Your Life

Another way the Universe may call to you is through the people in your life. I've found that every single person in your life—from the people you choose to associate with, to the family you were randomly born into, to the stranger you jostle with for a seat on the subway—is there for a reason. They are guiding you, teaching you, supporting you, perhaps showing you whom you don't want to be, connecting with you, redirecting you, challenging you, and pushing you toward change. Yes, the good, the bad, and the indifferent all play critical roles in your story and your journey through life. We can't always see the reason at the time, but at some point it is likely to be revealed.

Here's another example. When I was chief of staff in 2016, the president I supported was writing and launching a book. I didn't pay it much mind at the time, but four years later, when I had almost forty thousand words of my memoir written, I knew just whom to call for advice. He introduced me to my editor without hesitation. I later thanked him for not hanging up on me when he heard the title, but *of course* he didn't. This was meant to be part of my story. He was put in my life for a reason, and a good reason at that. Can you think of a mentor, colleague, or friend who feels like they were put in your life for a reason? People like this can help reaffirm that you are on the right path and should keep going in a particular direction.

On the flip side, there were people I worked with in my last corporate job who made my life absolutely miserable. They tarnished my name, threw me under the bus, land-grabbed, and steamrolled me. And you know what? I'm grateful. If my job had been rosy, I might have stayed. I might have missed out on my purpose. They were intentionally there to guide me out of my corporate career. While it hurt in the moment, and certainly isn't how anyone should treat a coworker, I now see how pivotal this actually was to my transformation. I could not have reinvented my life the way I did without this pain. What pain are you experiencing that is guiding you toward a pivot? A bad relationship? A toxic friendship? A bad business partnership? Pay attention to these signs and be ready to explore where you want to initiate change, which we'll discuss more in Chapter 3.

But how many of us are missing signs? Or misinterpreting the presence of others in our lives? I'd wager a large portion of the population, and for good reason. You're busy. You're distracted by the day-to-day grind and don't have time to recognize all that's going on and why it's happening. That was my problem when I was in corporate. In hindsight, I was given so many signs, but I never took the time to really evaluate them. This was mainly because they made me uncomfortable, and acting on them would require massive change in my life.

Here's what you can do if you need more help opening up to the signs in your life:

Know that the Universe is on your side. It's not trying to hide anything from you. This isn't a game or a scavenger hunt. By slowing down and being present to what the Universe is sharing, you'll become more in tune with the messages. Like a budding friendship, over time your trust in the Universe will grow.

Write things down. When you believe you've experienced a sign, take note. If the same sign keeps popping up or you're seeing similar patterns, surely this isn't a coincidence. Capture these thoughts and get ready to investigate them further.

Focus on simplicity. The Universe wants you to see the sign, so it will be as straightforward as possible. Keep an eye out for the simplest meaning of a message.

Tap into your gut feeling. Your intuition is an innate tool. It's there to protect you and keep you safe. Take advantage of it. We're so conditioned to tune out our gut reaction. Forget about the societal messages that want to silence your intuition, and turn up the volume on your Higher Power.

You may desire to change for the better, but that also means you need to feel empowered to make those changes. Part of the reason it took me so long to accept the idea of leaving the corporate world is because I had never felt empowered to leave that part of me behind. At this point you may see the signs and understand them but not feel empowered to follow through. Not to worry; you can overcome this just like I did.

If you're aware of the signs and you have a good, clear picture of what the Universe is telling you, you're ready to move on to Chapter 3. Signs without actions are useless. Chapter 3 will teach you—now that you understand that life is short and that you're being guided by the Universe to your purpose—how to confidently take strides in that direction.

Later we will talk about how the Universe can test you, but for the moment I want you to focus on learning to listen to and trust its guidance. The key now is for you to see the signs that are being sent to you in your life. Trust me, they are there. As Tony Robbins has pointed out, life is not happening *to* you, as it may seem, but *for* you. Embrace this concept, and your dream life is well on its way to you. And that's no woo-woo.

• •

Make It Happen

In this chapter's "Make It Happen" section, we're going to dive a bit deeper into the exercises I introduced you to in Chapter 1, specifically journaling and quiet time. The journal prompt that follows will help you think critically about signs you may have missed before, while the Quiet Time exercise will help you tune out all the chatter of the world around you and tune into yourself, which is one of the primary keys to listening out for these signs.

Journaling

What seems ambiguous at times may gain clarity over time, just as my signs did for me. Now you get to take some time to reflect on the signs in your life. Remember, something that seems bad on the surface may indeed be a blessing on further inspection. Take a moment to consider and write out answers to the following in your journal:

    ↪   What signs may I have missed in the past?

    ↪   How did a negative event actually work out in my favor?

⚬   What if I viewed this setback as the set*up* for a comeback? How would that change things?

⚬   What signs have I seen and embraced?

⚬   How did those signs steer me in the right direction?

⚬   How can I identify ways to be present to future signs as they come up?

⚬   What would I like to manifest in my life?

Once you start to see the signs, things will begin to line up for you, and you'll have more confidence to go for your goals. Additionally, if you've kept a journal for years, go back and read old entries. Note any similar feelings or threads that run through them. This can be helpful for noticing patterns and trends in your life, as well as trouble spots that flare up repeatedly.

Quiet Time

Sometimes it's hard to see or hear the signs because we have too many distractions. With our phones' notifications chiming every five seconds and at least our own schedule, if not our partner's and/or children's schedules, to balance, we rarely get any breaks to hear or receive the signs.
It's important to be intentional about creating quiet time and reducing noise. The difference between this exercise and Sitting in Silence from Chapter 1 is that, here, you can enjoy some music or the natural sounds from your environment. You're actively and intentionally slowing down so you can be more present to the signs you're being sent.

Here are some ideas for creating a conducive environment to receive your signs:

- Limit social media use to thirty minutes a day

- Take two days off a week from TV, including the news

- Work out with earbuds in but nothing playing on them

- Drive to work in complete silence

- Take a nature hike

- Meditate—even five minutes can be enough to experience a breakthrough

- Pray

- Take a quiet bath with some candles and spa music

- Go to bed thirty minutes earlier and lie still in the dark

- Read scripture

Chapter 3

Commit to Change

*Stepping onto a brand-new path is difficult, but
not more difficult than remaining in a situation,
which is not nurturing to the whole woman.*

—MAYA ANGELOU

During my "Oh Shit!" Moment phase, I was toxic, to say
the least. I was in so much emotional pain that I wanted
everyone else to know it. This wasn't because I enjoyed being
a downer; it was a disguised cry for help. I was failing as
a mom, drowning in work, and jaded about life. Pure venom
ran through my blood most days. I was so busy being angry
with the world, but the only person I had to be mad at was

myself. The fact that I had let myself down felt too hard to deal with.

Though this all came to a head during my thirties, I'd been feeling this way for quite some time. I had quit acting only five years into pursuing my dream, and I'd applied for a job in corporate America. It was supposed to be temporary, a quick money-making scheme, so I could go back to acting fulltime and ditch waiting tables. I wasn't supposed to stay there, and yet I had sold out for money and status. (Coach purses and a BCBG wardrobe, to be honest.)

Before I knew it, time had flown by, and I felt like I'd forfeited my precious freedom and flexibility for good. I'd extinguished my creativity before it ever had a chance to ignite into a blaze. Beyond that, I had sacrificed my family for my work. No one made me do it. I did it to myself.

Maybe this sounds familiar to you. Are there choices you regret? Decisions for which you want a do-over?

It's okay if the answer is yes. At some point we all hit a wall. (I'm guessing you're there since you're reading this book.) Eventually, we can no longer keep going in the same direction we have been. When I hit my wall, I had spent the last fifteen years in the passenger seat of life, letting things happen to me. I wanted to get back in control of my destiny. The only way to do that? Jump in the driver's seat. If I wanted to make things happen *for* myself, rather than witness things happening *to* me, change was going to be unavoidable.

In this chapter, I'll share with you why it's hard for many women to change, how to approach change in a way that won't overwhelm or scare you out of taking the necessary steps, and how to keep yourself motivated once you begin to change. Additionally, if you understand what the typical cycle of change looks like, and know what pitfalls and backslides might happen once you start to change, then you can be more prepared and possibly even avoid those detours altogether.

Even though change can be difficult, it's absolutely worth it in the end. Why? Because you'll be living your true purpose. You'll finally feel the fulfillment you've been craving. Sound good? Let's go.

Why Change Feels Hard

Consider the Nike slogan: Just do it. Can you believe it? A sneaker company had the keys to change the whole time: Just freaking do it. And yet, we don't.

Why do we stay stuck? Because we're afraid of the C-word. *No, not that one.* This one: change! For many women, as soon as they think or hear this word, all hope of a different circumstance flies out the window.

Here's the thing about change: it can feel scary. You're stepping into the unknown and trusting that you have read the signs from the Universe correctly. The fact that change involves a leap of faith can make even positive change feel difficult and terrifying, so people often talk themselves out of it. *What if I change so much that my friends don't want to talk to me anymore? What if I take money, effort, and time to change and nothing improves? What if my partner doesn't like the new me?* The status quo may be awful, but it's an awfulness you know, which makes it a weird kind of comfortable. And so, you wallow deeper into the mire.

No judgment for any wallowing! We've all been there. I'm here to honor those feelings *and* give you the support you need to make the change(s) anyway. Trust me—you really can do it.

Enacting Positive Change Through SMART Goals

Keep in mind that change can mean different things to different people. There are big changes (e.g., moving your family to another country) and small changes (e.g., spreading kindness by smiling more at your job). There are even microchanges so small that no one else would notice (e.g., drinking an extra glass of water each day).

Let's discuss how to set actionable goals you can reach with positive change. By this point, you might be starting to think of some concrete things that you'd like to change in your life. Good! Now is a great time to start considering your goals. Committing to change is great, but we need to know exactly what it is we're committing to if we want a chance at succeeding. After all, if you back out of your driveway but don't know your destination, you're just wasting gas circling the block, aren't you?

Even if this still feels a little fuzzy, take a stab at writing your goals out. We'll talk about this more in Part 3's "Document Your Goal," so for now, just know that a goal left in your head is only a dream. According to research from the University of Scranton, only 8 percent of people achieve their dreams.

I'm not a math whiz, but those aren't great odds. I don't mean to burst any bubbles here. Really, what I'm telling you is good news. According to Dr. Gail Matthews, a psychologist and career coach at the Dominican University of California, you're 42 percent more likely to achieve your goals when you write them down. All the more reason to get them etched on paper!

Writing goals is a bit of an art. Don't worry; you don't need to be Picasso or anything, but there is definitely a formula at play here. Perhaps you've heard of SMART goals before. There's a reason every good coach talks about them—because they work! A SMART goal is a goal expressed (or, better yet, written!) in a way that is Specific, Measurable, Achievable, Relevant, and Timely. Sounds easy enough, yet if any one of these components is missing, you could be setting yourself up for disappointment. We don't want that!

When I sit down with my clients to help them craft their goals, they almost always show up with something too vague. *I want to be a better mom*, for instance. I can see why that comes up a lot. Most of my clients are high-achieving women who work demanding jobs. It makes sense that they desire a better connection with their children, but simply saying "I want to be a better mom" doesn't give us much to go on in terms of the actions that need to be taken to reach that point. For one thing, two women's definitions of being a better mom can vary wildly, and the steps you'll need to take to show up for more soccer games are different from the steps you'll need to take to listen more actively to your children at the dinner table. Let's run this currently vague dream through the

SMART process together so you can see how it shapes up to be a viable, achievable goal.

Specific: I want to spend more quality time one-on-one with my child. (This shows how you're defining being a better mom.)

Measurable: I will spend at least thirty minutes a day Monday through Friday with my child. (We can measure if it happened or not.)

Achievable: I will make this happen by carving out time in my calendar. (We can see where the available time slots are, or what could be replaced by your quality time, e.g., TV time, and how the Measurable goal is achievable.)

Relevant: Yes. (As a mom it's very common to want to enjoy time with your children while they still live at home.)

Timely/Time-bound: I will implement this change by the end of the month and be consistent with it until the end of the school year. (We'll know whether you met the goal by the end of the month, and you'll be held accountable for doing it through the remainder of the school year.)

Voilà! By taking a vague resolution like being a better mom and transforming it into a SMART goal, you're not only making it more likely that you'll achieve your dream you're also giving the Universe fuel to support you. Being a better mom is a hard concept for the Universe to bring to fruition, but knowing it needs to create space for thirty minutes each day so that you can play or read with your child is a lot more concrete. Further, your brain will see your desired change and help you manifest it. If you're feeling really brave, grab someone and share your goals with them! In coaching we call this an accountability partner, which simply means anyone who can support you in achieving your goals, whether by being your cheerleader or nudging you to follow through.

Again, this is just a primer for how to achieve your dreams through positive change. Some of you might be feeling like you still aren't sure what you want your goals to be. That's okay; the following chapters will help you through the exploration phase, where you'll create a clearer picture of your desired life. Additionally, there might be some roadblocks holding you back, which we'll discuss shortly.

How to Kickstart Change

Despite their fear of change, a lot of my clients find themselves in a situation where changing is eventually easier than the pain of staying the same. However, instead of making dramatic decisions overnight, their more successful attempts at change happen gradually over time. In my therapeutic experience, the changes that stick, the ones that help a person move confidently in the direction of their goals, have two things in common:

   ↺   These changes all start with mental rewiring.

   ↺   One change has a domino effect on others.

Mental Rewiring

We've spoken a bit about mental rewiring already, especially when we discussed having a gratitude practice. Seeking out the positive in our lives helps us to see more positive more readily—*and* to be ready to hear messages from the Universe.

In the same way, rewiring is an important initial step to making change that sticks.

Take my "Oh Shit!" Moment panic attacks for instance. That nightly ritual went on for several months. It got so bad that I dreaded being alone in the dark because I knew my thoughts of death could surface at any moment. One night I drew a line in the sand. Enough was enough. I wanted my power back. There I was, face to face with myself in the bathroom mirror again, this time just before bed.

> *Do I really want to live like this any longer? No. This ends tonight. From now on, whenever I go into the bathroom in the middle of the night, I'm replacing the negative thought immediately with a different thought. Any thought. Anything other than contemplating death. It's the only way I can think to break the cycle. I have to try it.*

That night around 3:30 a.m., I woke up as usual. Instead of using the lowest setting on the dimmer switch, I chose the middle one. Maybe more light would keep the thoughts at bay. It strained my eyes, and they squinted shut, leaving the smallest possible opening between my lashes to find the toilet.

So far, so good.

…I wonder how long it takes for worms to get into your casket.

Nope! Not doing this. Look, there's a crack in that tile over there. Better get Danny to patch that up this weekend. My goodness, when is the last time we swept the floor? I'm shedding like a corgi around here! How do I even have any hair left on my head? I bet I don't look so good bald.

Before I knew it, my word vomit had preoccupied my mind, and I was exiting the bathroom without a hitch. Night after night, I did the same thing. As soon as the thought hit, I went into my monologue.

Geez, I better paint these nails. They look terrible, so chipped. Tomorrow is going to be a busy day. Lots to prepare for work, and I need to plan for my trip to Austin soon. I need to go shopping for a new dress to wear in the booth. I'm glad we painted the walls gray. So much better than that hideous wallpaper.

Eventually, I would go into the bathroom and not even have a thought about death that required me to come up with random thoughts. Eventually, I could use the lowest setting on the dimmer switch again. Eventually, I had my life back.

All this time I had been using a technique; I just didn't know it. What technique, you ask?

Rewiring the brain. As I came to find out later, through my life coaching certification, there is something called Hebb's law, which states that neurons that fire together wire together. In other words, the more we do a task, the better we get at it. Makes sense, right? My son had a hard time learning to tie his shoes, but the more he practiced, the better he got. Eventually the neurons all fired together to make him be able to do this task on autopilot. That's a positive example of the brain's wiring. What other positive examples can you think of in your life? A baby learning to walk? Learning to ride a bike? Picking up a new hobby like scrapbooking or tennis?

At first, I was strengthening my neurons in a bad way: so that I had negative thoughts every time I entered the bathroom. Sometimes, for change to be effective, you have to actually change the way the synapses in your brain fire. By retraining my brain to think of something different, I was actually breaking that connection and rewiring my brain to have a different response. I was retraining my brain so that I didn't think about death in the bathroom at night anymore. How cool is that?

What's even cooler is that you can rewire your brain too. Is there anything that comes to mind that you'd like to rewire? Jot it down so you don't forget. Spoiler alert: you'll give it a try in the "Make It Happen" section shortly.

The Domino Effect

Distracting myself from my mortality with random thoughts was obviously a good first step, but rewiring my brain alone wasn't going to be a big enough change to fully improve the quality of my life or to get me closer to living my purpose. Rewiring was critical to do, yes, because my panic attacks were distracting symptoms of what was really causing me discomfort, but now I needed to make active, practical changes to cut the cause out at its root. If death did come, which I couldn't control, then I wanted to live a life I was proud of.

Instead of living in my head, which I knew from my middle-of-the-night panic attacks was prone to making up information and stories, I got smart and started seeking facts to help me make these other important changes.

I began by making a list of the biggest changes I wanted to make and scored them on a scale from 1 to 5. The score denoted the positive level of impact that change would have on my life, with 1 meaning it would have little to no impact and 5 meaning it would have a significant impact.

Then I assessed whether I was ready to make those changes right away. For example, I knew I wanted out of corporate, but I wasn't ready to walk in and give my two weeks' notice yet. However, since it would have a big impact on my happiness if I could make that change, resigning from my marketing job scored high on my list of important changes to make.

One of the reasons I was so scared to leave my job was the financial aspect. Walking away from the security and regular income corporate America offered me and my family was not easy. Could I leave a six-figure paycheck behind to pursue my dreams? Often, we make decisions based on information we think we know or something we've heard in the past. A college professor once told me I'd always be poor. Subconsciously I think I had carried that sting around for years, trying to prove her wrong. Was I poor? Had I made good financial decisions? I needed a professional to help me discern the truth, so I met with a financial planner to get concrete information.

Turns out my husband and I were crushing it. We found out we could retire at age fifty if we wanted to. When the financial planner said we had enough assets that we should get a trust, I almost fell out of my chair. *Me? I am raising trust fund kids? How is that possible? Little old me, the dance major. This gives me so much power that I didn't know I had.*

Of course, I thought he was mistaken at first and asked him to recheck the numbers a few times, but it was fact. Now, I was free to make financial decisions that I didn't know were possible. I actually didn't need to work so many hours. I could comfortably take a pay cut while I built up my coaching business and not stress about paying my bills at the same time. Worst case, I might have to retire at fifty-five. I could live with that.

Yet when I got those concrete answers, like clockwork, here came the fear. *What will change mean for my life? My bank account? My status?*

I did my best not to give in to the fear, reminding myself it's a normal byproduct of change. Instead, I saw that meeting with the financial planner as the first domino: a single action that triggered a chain reaction leading to further changes in my life. See, just as pushing one domino causes a ripple effect and sets off a sequence of falling dominos, initiating one change can create momentum and make subsequent changes easier. I used that first step to knock down one more domino, then another and another.

One of the most important questions I asked myself when a change felt scary was, *What's the worst that could happen by making this change?* That question was so freeing for me. Nothing I was committing to was permanent. I could always go back to a job in corporate America. It wasn't like I was deciding whether to end someone's life. It was all reversible.

It was interesting to find, though, that in the midst of this "it's all reversible" pep talk, as I started to make a few changes, it became easier to make more and more changes. It really is like a set of dominos; once you push the first one down and each subsequent one gathers momentum, the rest fall into place more and more easily.

One of the biggest changes I made was moving with my husband and kids from New Jersey to South Carolina. Without all the previous changes I'd made (leaving corporate, starting a business), I'm not sure I could have made this change so easily. Not everyone is willing to make this type of move, but when I began to really evaluate what I wanted out of life, the hustle and bustle of the city was no longer it. Financially, we had worked really hard not to live above our means and saved as much as possible. Because of the market, we could pay off our mortgage and buy our new home with cash, which took a ton of pressure off my new business. Sure, we were leaving our extended family up north, which was difficult. At the same time, we were gaining a better life for ourselves and our kids, which was priceless.

What could be your first domino? What stories are you telling yourself that are holding you back? Get the facts and begin making the changes you desire.

The Benefit of Starting Small

Making changes requires you to be very detailed with what you want, what you will no longer tolerate (i.e., "the nonnegotiables"), and what you can be flexible with. After I left my corporate job, my first business coach had me map out my dream life right from the beginning. I knew I didn't want to work on Fridays any longer, so she encouraged me to put a block in my calendar on those days. I also knew I wanted the mornings free for workouts and taking the kids to school and afternoons free to pick them up. I blocked out all of these windows to create my dream life.

But, right on cue, old habits from my workaholic days were creeping back into my business life. I would get a request to meet with a new client, look at my calendar, and see Friday wide open. *I'll just slot in a few calls this week*, I'd think. *I really want to meet with these people.* I could reason all I wanted, but I was already letting go of the promises I made to myself. It took my kids and husband calling me out at dinner one night to get me to stick with my "No Work on Fridays" rule.

Part of what made this difficult was how big the change felt. Taking a whole day off was jarring, so I committed to a smaller shift. I backed down from taking the whole day off and got used to a half day. For the next three months, I focused on honoring Friday off from noon onwards. Spoiler alert: I was suddenly able to follow through and take that time off. Eventually, I was strong enough to take the entire day. Adding another four hours of "me" time was an easy transition because I had set myself up for success.

Now my Fridays are sacred time for me and my well-being. Sometimes I nap, sometimes I do an extra-long workout, or I might read a book. Often I will volunteer, meet with my middle school mentee, or give back to the community in other ways. It's my day to use how I see fit, as long as it isn't working on my business.

If making a big change scares you, what smaller version of that change could you start with?

The Cycle of Change

As you grip the wheel of your metaphorical driver's seat and commit more deeply to change, you may really like the feel of it. There's a surge of power and control that you likely haven't felt in a long time. Like many experiences in life, the more time you spend in the change process, the more comfortable and confident you'll become with it.

I've found this to be true for myself and my clients. As such, I've found there is a typical cycle that many of us experience when initiating a change. I've outlined it below, using smoking cessation as an example:

Awareness: You understand that there is a problem and begin to contemplate making a change to address or alleviate it. For instance, your doctor runs some tests and tells you that you must stop smoking or you're going to develop lung cancer. You recognize it's a problem and start researching ways to quit.

Consideration: You become more serious about the change and begin to actively investigate solutions. You look at the nicotine patch, gum replacements, and quitting on the spot.

Commitment: You have enough information to feel relatively comfortable with making the change. You begin to take small steps in the right direction. You decide to start with gum replacements to avoid potential side effects. At the same time, you decide to start walking more to improve your lung function.

Excitement: You're excited about the possibilities and enjoy the changes you're experiencing in your life. You feel great the first few days, follow through on your commitments, and enjoy not smelling like smoke—maybe for the first time in years!

Fear: As soon as you hit a challenge or roadblock, though, you become worried you made the wrong move. You even romanticize your old way of living, seeking ways to return to your former self. Something goes wrong at work, and a coworker sends you a nasty email. Your automatic stress response is to walk outside and have a smoke. You wish you could just have one more cigarette, so you find a coworker to give you one.

Awareness: You once again become acutely aware of why you made the change in the first place. You light up outside and instantly remember why you quit. You know smoking won't make your work problem go away, so you toss the butt on the ground.

Recommitment: You more fully commit to making the necessary changes and following through. You go back to your desk and pop a piece of gum, even more committed not to smoke again.

Smoking is a fairly easy-to-follow example, but not every change will be this straightforward. I've had clients with more complicated changes, like deciding to divorce a partner, leave a company where they've worked for over twenty years, pull a child from their school to get them necessary support and resources elsewhere, or even create distance between themselves and a toxic family member.

The change cycle can be repeated any number of times, with each stage varying in length depending on that particular instance's circumstances. Hopefully you can avoid relapses through awareness of how this cycle works. However, I've failed a few times, had false starts, fallen off the wagon, as it were, and had to pick myself up, recommit, and try again. You might not nail change on the first try, but that doesn't mean you should throw in the towel and walk away. We all experience fear when we're making a change. It's par for the course, so learn to accept it instead of fighting it. Your journey will be much easier with that understanding.

Rewarding Yourself for Positive Change

Remember our discussion of extrinsic and intrinsic motivation in Chapter 1? Reward systems are a great extrinsic motivator that keeps you going along your change journey even when it'd be easier to give up.

How does a reward system, whether you've consciously created it or not, work? Essentially, you take an action, like working out on the treadmill, and then reward yourself, perhaps with a delicious chocolate protein shake, afterward. By rewiring your brain to associate your good behavior (working out) with a reward (the chocolate shake), you've made sure you want to exercise—even on days when you're exhausted—so you can enjoy that tasty treat.

As we saw before, dopamine is a key component to our happiness, so it's no surprise it plays a role here too. When it's exposed to a stimulus that is rewarding, like wine, a yummy treat, or a new pair of shoes, the brain responds by releasing an increased amount of dopamine, the main neurotransmitter associated with rewards and pleasure. As we leverage our rewards, we are strengthening our neural pathways. We are telling our brain, *I take this action, and you get rewarded with this pleasurable thing.*

However, not all reward systems are created equal. You may be creating a negative reward system without realizing it. Negative reward systems that are astonishingly socially acceptable include downtime in front of the television, spending outside of your budget ("Hey, it's your day! Treat yourself!"), and associating alcohol with celebration. (More on this later.) Dopamine is dopamine, and your brain will take it where it can get it.

So, what can you do if you're at risk of—or already have—a poor reward system? First, ask yourself: *Is this behavior serving me?* There is no judgment here; what serves one person may not serve another. It's not a matter of right or wrong. It's a matter of what makes your life better. What makes you a happier, more productive person? Ask yourself, *Does it get me closer to or further from my dreams? Closer to or further from fulfilling my destiny?*

If the answer is "further from," it may be time to recalibrate your reward system.

The Pitfalls and Backslides of Change

As you follow through on your desired changes, there may still be demons that need to be expunged. Old habits tend to rear their ugly heads in the "Fear" stage of the change cycle; they love to make a resurgence any time you experience discomfort with the change process.

Just as my changes would start to lead to results, I would often suffer from self-doubt and lack of self-worth, which led to a few self-sabotaging demons. These problematic safe spaces were:

- Alcohol
- Workaholism
- Prioritizing work over family
- Stress eating

Though I refer to this list as "my demons" now, at the time, they were like old friends. I was comfortably numb when I was drinking or stress eating. They were my crutches, my coping mechanisms to get through the good times and the bad.

During the summer of 2019, my husband and I found ourselves in a nightly ritual. We would get the kids to bed, turn the TV to the news station, pour ourselves a drink, and then scream for the next hour about how everything was going to shit. At first I felt like I was informed and more educated about what was going on in the world; no harm there. But an hour slowly turned into ninety minutes. Then I'd stay up way too late and find I'd spent over two hours glued to the tube—and consumed three glasses of wine to boot.

My husband and I would complain about how we didn't have any time for things we wanted to do, individually or together, and yet we spent ten hours a week dazed by the TV—hmm, looks like plenty of time to me! Eventually we recognized two changes needed to be made: we needed to limit our time in front of the TV, and we needed to reduce our alcohol intake. Of course, drinking was also why I was waking up in the middle of the night to go to the bathroom. (Pro tip: if you stop drinking twenty-four ounces of liquid before bed, you'll stop waking up and having panic attacks at 3 a.m.) It was so simple, but I had never made the connection before. Plus, by not watching the news every night, my husband and I had more time to work on our relationship, and I had more time to write my book and launch my business. It was a win-win.

Fast-forward to a year later. I was now on the cusp of creating my dream life as an author and a life coach. My husband and I had more time together and were watching less television… *but* I was still getting sucked into drinking regularly. I wanted to celebrate everything with a drink. Got a client? Have a drink. Updated the website? Toast to my accomplishment. Finished a chapter of the book? Indulge in a cocktail. But I noticed a pattern: every time I drank, I got lazy and things fell behind schedule. (Remember, I said we'd come back to this!) I needed a new reward system, one that didn't deplete me or throw me off track.

Personally, alcohol no longer served me. Once I identified behaviors that no longer supported my goals and dreams,

I had to make a commitment to change. I had to declare it. Write it down. Say it out loud. Tell others who would support me. I had to let my brain know I meant business.

I went from drinking three glasses of wine a day, seven days a week, to occasionally having *a* drink with friends or if my husband and I had a special occasion. Drinking during the week at home, Monday through Thursday, was off the table. I felt a million times better and was shocked by how much more time I had to devote to my family and my business. Plus, I lost weight and felt the best I had, physically and mentally, in years. I've come a long way and committed to the change I needed to improve my life. Crazy, what a little change can do for you.

I know it's easy to read about my change and think, *Well, that worked for you, but you don't know my situation.*

I used to think so, too, when other people would shove what I thought of as their "pipe dreams of change" in my face. It's easy to dismiss the changes you could make to your lifestyle as "hard" or "impossible" when you feel stuck. It may be hard to see how this could ever work for your situation. As you read this, you may even be coming up with all the excuses as to why this style of change only works for me and my clients and why it wouldn't work for you! Yet, everywhere you look, you're seeing people bust the status quo, listen to signs from the Universe, and commit to change. Why not you too?

You can't change the past, but you do have a choice for your future. You can either spend your whole life blaming everyone else, or you can buck up and commit to change. I can tell you with profound certainty that the former option will yield you no success and will likely make things worse. The sooner you buy into this realization and employ the latter, the sooner you can start living your dream life.

Which will it be? You get to choose right now. Seriously, what's it going to be? If you're ready to choose change, write it down and say it out loud: *I choose change.* Bottom line: if I can do it, so can you. What life changes do you want to make today? As Nike would say, just do it.

Next, we'll shift to Part 2, which will help you develop the skills, mindset, and habits you need to support positive change and maintain it for the long haul. For now, let's roll up our sleeves to "Make It Happen" when it comes to committing to change.

• •

Make It Happen

Journaling

Remember, back in the meat of this chapter, when I encouraged you to specify the part of your life you wanted to change? Now, take some time to list this out in greater detail. Then identify how you will stay committed to this change. Armed with this information, you'll be ready to move forward. By now you know the drill: don't self-edit during the journaling process.

Maybe you've identified that you need a new job, but you're worried about money so you talk yourself out of writing that down. Maybe you consider a divorce, but aren't sure how you can afford it, so you leave it off. Maybe you want to start working out, but you worry about what people at the gym will think about your body, so you keep it in your head. At the moment, you're dreaming, you're getting honest with yourself. You shouldn't feel any pressure to make all of these changes at once. We'll refine this when we get to the EDIT™ Methodology in Part 3. For now, answer the following questions in your journal:

⊘   What are the biggest changes I need to make?

- What small changes can I make now to prepare me for the larger changes?

- What behaviors no longer serve me?

- How can I ensure I give these behaviors up?

- What changes will be the hardest to make, and why?

- What are my initial SMART goals?

- How will I hold myself accountable for making these changes?

- Who can be my accountability partner during this time of transition and change?

Change Diary

Change is easier when we have something to compare it to or a past experience that anchors you to the ability to make another change. With this in mind, I like to have my clients create a change diary. It's a log of all the changes they've made in the past and the positive outcome(s) they've experienced as a result.

Start by reflecting on all the big changes you've made in your life. You should have a pretty big list if you're giving yourself credit for all the changes you've been through. Go back as far as you can remember. Here's a small excerpt from my list:

- Took a ballet class

- Went away to college

- Quit smoking

- Left my job in sales for a training position

- Was let go from my marketing job

Now, note the positive impact you experienced as a result of those changes. It may be surprising to realize even changes you thought were bad have had positive impacts. By reflecting on these past changes, you've got proof you can make new changes from your spot in the driver's seat:

- Took a ballet class – Although this was really hard at first, I ended up becoming a better dancer as a result.

- Went away to college – I learned how to live on my own, use a checkbook, do laundry, and I acquired other important life skills that I rely on every day.

- Quit smoking – I learned I had the willpower to stop. I had more endurance, felt better, and no longer smelled like smoke.

- Left my job in sales for a training position – I had no experience as a trainer but ended up being one of the best in my department and really enjoyed my work.

- Was let go from my marketing job – I ended up getting the nudge I needed to follow my heart and finish my memoir.

Accountability Partner

Need an accountability partner, but feel your changes are too personal or embarrassing to share with your friends? It's nice to talk about your problems, brainstorm solutions, and discuss new and exciting goals with unbiased third parties who are going through similar situations. Join my Facebook group, Successful Working Women Rocking Reinvention, for additional accountability:

www.facebook.com/groups/workingwomenrockingreinvention

Part 2
Getting Unstuck

Chapter 4

Turn Inward

*Your vision will become clear only when you look
into your heart. Who looks inside awakens.*

—CARL JUNG, *LETTERS, VOL. 1*

Once you've had your "Oh Shit!" Moment, seen the signs from the Universe, and committed to change, it's time to make your dream life a reality. Acknowledging that you're ready for a change and actually making a change are not one and the same, though. It's time to outline the key steps to making your transformation long-lasting.

How do I know these steps will work? I know because these are the exact steps I used to get out of my midlife slump, and they are the exact same steps I use with my clients every day. Are there other ways to get to the same end result? Probably. You could always marry into money or win the lottery, *then* quit your day job, but even if either of those goals could be reached strategically, they still might not make you happy—especially when everyone starts asking you for handouts. My suggestion is to follow these steps in the subsequent chapters to create a life you truly love:

1. Turn Inward
2. Rekindle Your Passions
3. Let's Get Spiritual
4. Make Over Your Mindset
5. Create Unshakable Confidence
6. Find a Bigger Purpose
7. Own Your Power

We'll explore each of these steps in depth in the following chapters. You may find yourself gravitating toward some topics more than others; that's natural. Everyone is going to require a different level of support depending on their unique circumstances. That's why my one-on-one coaching programs are custom-built for each client. Since I don't know which areas you need the most help in, I'll present all of the steps for you to devour and implement as needed. For now, let's focus on Step 1: Turn Inward.

What does "turn inward" even mean? To me, turning inward is looking deep within yourself, traveling to the depths of your soul, for the answers to your biggest questions:

- What do I want out of life?
- Who am I?
- What makes me happy?
- What are my core values?
- What is my full potential, and how can I reach it?
- What will I regret not doing while I'm here on Earth?

Turning inward to discover your purpose can help you gain much-needed clarity and direction in life, leading to greater self-awareness and self-acceptance. This can result in increased confidence, fulfillment, and a greater sense of meaning in life. Who doesn't want that?

Having a clear sense of purpose can help you make informed choices and prioritize your time and energy, leading to a more balanced and satisfying life. As women, we often find ourselves pulled in multiple directions, trying to balance our responsibilities at home, at work, and in our relationships. In this fast-paced world, it's easy to lose sight of what truly matters to us and of what our purpose in life is. However, taking the time to turn inward and reflect on our passions, values, and goals can be incredibly empowering and life-changing.

When you turn inward, you allow yourself to tap into your inner wisdom and intuition and to get in touch with your authentic self. This can help you gain a clearer understanding of what drives you, what you're passionate about, and what you truly want out of life.

Turning inward also suggests a break from or rejection of outward forces. It means putting less stock in what those around you say about you or what they think you *should* do. (Not everyone comes out and bosses us around. If you're a people pleaser, recovering or active, this may even mean putting less stock in what *you think* people are thinking about you!) For all of us, turning inward means seeking less validation from others and instead trusting yourself to come up with the best answers—the answers that are true for you.

The Negative Impact of Social Media (and Social Circles!) on Turning Inward

In a society that craves outward attention and validation, the notion of turning inward can feel like a foreign concept to many. Just look at the rise of TikTok or any other social media platform to see how desperate our society is for outward approval: moms posting their perfect toddlers in matching outfits, working women 'gramming about their work trips abroad, all in an attempt to impress others and see how many likes and comments they can get. And when we don't get as many likes as we think we should, we start to question our worth.

Too many of us are victims of the comparison game, comparing our everyday lives to our friends' highlight reels. I've had so many clients complain that they feel they are missing out on life or aren't as successful as they *should* be by now, all because of what they've seen on social media. Yet if we were truly turning inward, none of this would matter. You might be asking yourself, *So, what's the answer? To get off social media altogether?* Not necessarily. But turning inward does require us to be intentional about how we use social media and how we contextualize what we see when we're online.

We should also keep in mind that not all validation is sought through social media. Sometimes we seek input and guidance from our peers, friends, family, or other respected sources. For instance, my mom recently called me from the salon with foils in her hair.

"Should I cut my hair into a bob?" she asked.

Anyone else would have probably launched straight into all the reasons why she should or shouldn't do that. Being a coach, I just had to probe deeper.

"What do *you* want to do?"

"I don't know. That's why I called you."

"Well, what makes you want to cut it short?"

"It's getting a little cumbersome to manage at this length, and I think it's weighing me down. What do you think? Would it look good short?"

"It doesn't matter what I think, Mom. It's about what you will like when you look in the mirror."

This back-and-forth questioning went on for a few minutes until I made the suggestion of a compromise: "Why not cut it to the shoulders? If you want to go shorter, you can always have your stylist keep cutting."

She got off the phone frustrated she still had to make the decision, but I knew it was the right way to handle her question. I couldn't tell her what she should do with her hair. Only she had those answers. She ultimately went with the suggestion to go shoulder-length and ended up stopping at that point. The result? She was happy with her hair and got what she wanted: something easier to manage that looked healthy all the time.

My mom's hair quandary is an example of a relatively small question. But can you imagine doing this—phoning a friend or loved one—for all your big life changes? It sounds impossible, yet so many people do just that! They ask others how they should be living, whom they should date, what career would be best for them. Then, if it doesn't work out, at least they have someone else to blame. But then they're right back at square one. Better to take the time to turn inward now and end up with a life you love.

The Problem with "What Should I Do?"

When I was at the height of my midlife crisis, I wanted so badly for someone, anyone, to give me answers to my big questions. Every chance I got, I'd ask other people what they thought I should do next. I was desperately searching for the key to happiness, which I was convinced someone else had but was hiding from me. I also spent significant time looking for answers in the bottom of a wine bottle, as you've already heard. It seemed I had convinced myself the more I drank, the closer I'd get to finding my purpose. The opposite was actually true. I was taking myself further and further off course. We'll discuss self-sabotaging in more detail later.

But here's the problem with asking others what you should be doing: the use of the word *should*. "What should I do?" we say. Well, *should* according to whom? Who makes the rules for your life? Hopefully you do, although maybe that's part of the reason why you're reading this book—because you realize you aren't in control of your destiny yet. If a decision were something you truly desired, without the push of outside forces, you wouldn't say *should*; you'd say it's something you want to do or get to do.

For example, if you said, "I should go back to school and get my master's degree," I would ask, "What makes you think you should do that?" This conversation could go in a multitude of directions, so I can't capture every scenario, but you might respond by saying something like, "Everyone in my family has their master's. I'm the only one who doesn't." That would be a clear sign this isn't something you inherently want to do but that you feel pressured to do. In my experience, women often feel pressure to conform to societal expectations and norms, which can lead us to prioritize external validation over our own needs and desires.

On the flip side you might say, "I have always wanted to get my master's, but I haven't felt financially stable until now. I also know I will earn a lot more at my company once the degree is complete, so there is a promising return on investment." That sounds a lot more like someone who actually wants to go through with getting a graduate degree.

In that case I'd invite you to change your language. Your new statement would be, "I *want* to go back to school and get my master's." Just that subtle change has a lot of big implications down the road, such as keeping you intrinsically motivated when the road gets rocky.

The second reason why asking people what you should do may not be helpful is they only know what you've already done. When I lost my B2B marketing job at an energy company, I called a CEO friend to tell him about my newfound freedom. At the time, I was interested in potentially starting a podcast, and since he had a podcast of his own, I thought this would be an excellent opportunity to pick his brain. But before I could tell him about my new idea to become a podcasting life coach, he started spouting off job ideas. Of course, all of his suggestions were to apply for more B2B marketing jobs—exactly what I didn't want! Any frustration I experienced in that moment was not his fault. How could he have known I wanted to make a change? I was finally able to explain my new life goal, and he made a key introduction to an established female coach, who ended up becoming my first business coach. The point is, if you only ask others what they think you *should* do and never consider your wants and needs, you'll be on a first-class flight to Miserableville. Not fun.

Even now, people want to tell me what I should be doing in my business. *Karin, you need to be on TikTok. Karin, you need to write a sequel to* The Ins and Outs of My Vagina. While I appreciate the advice and know it comes from a good place, it's not what I want to do. It's not what's in my heart when I turn inward, so I politely thank them and move on. You can do the same with unsolicited advice in your life.

How to Turn Inward

Instead of seeking social approval for our actions and choices, we want to take an intimate trip into the depths of our being in order to uncover our truest thoughts, feelings, wants, and desires—not to mention our biggest fears, regrets, worries, and weaknesses. Turning inward won't always be roses. There will surely be some painful moments. Perhaps you'll turn over some rocks you wish you had never looked under. But those hidden feelings need to come to light for you to move forward and get closer to living your purpose. Regardless of what comes up for you in this process, you'll be so glad you took the time to do this work. It will become the foundation of everything you do next.

So, how exactly do we turn inward? I'm sure you're eager to get started, but I want to point out that if this isn't something you've done in a long time or don't do regularly, it can be challenging at first. You may not be sure if some of the thoughts and feelings you notice are *actually* your thoughts or if they are messages you've received from others that you've convinced yourself are your own beliefs. This is a more common issue I see in my clients than you'd think. It can be awkward to pause and reflect on what you want, especially if you're always running a hundred miles an hour and can't sit still for more than five minutes. Or, for those who are mothers, who have put their entire identity into their children, it can feel strange to suddenly remember what makes you light up. You may feel like you don't even have any desires or dreams at this time. Remember, women are often caretakers and tend to prioritize the needs of others over our own, leading us to neglect our self-discovery process. You have dreams; they're under there somewhere—we just have to find and unearth them.

So, yes, turning inward takes time. It means becoming more mindful of your body and the signals it's sending you. *Am I always tired and feeling low energy? Why could that be?* Noticing what ails you or what makes you feel great will give you additional insights into what's working in your life. As I've mentioned, I was so stressed out in the latter part of my corporate career that I began grinding my teeth at night. My husband would shake me awake and alert me to my behavior, hoping it would stop the horrible noise, but of course, as soon as I dozed off, I'd be right back to unknowingly grinding again. This was a huge signal to me that something was wrong and the mounting stress was becoming problematic.

One of my clients, Brenda, also experienced signals from her body during one of our coaching periods. Remember how I mentioned that the Universe will sometimes test you in Chapter 2? Well, this was one such test. Brenda had decided to leave the corporate rat race to pursue an advanced degree in arts education. She was already about halfway through her master's program when she received an opportunity for a directorial role at one of the biggest media companies in New York. Was the Universe sending her a sign, or was it testing her conviction for her new path? I guided her through the process, inviting her to listen to how her body responded as she read through the job description. She noticed immediately that she felt anxious and nauseous as she combed through the assignments and responsibilities of the role. It was indeed a test, and by turning inward she was more committed than ever to continue pursuing her path as an art educator. It was a proud moment for both of us.

If you'd like to build up a practice that helps you more easily turn inward, the two tools that have been most useful for me are journaling and meditation.

Journaling

Can you tell journaling is one of my favorite processes? It's such a freeing exercise because it's safe—just between you, the paper, and your thoughts. No one else ever has to read it or know what you were thinking. It's also incredibly insightful. You gain so much knowledge about your true desires during the process.

Here's a concrete example of what I mean from my personal journal:

7/10/2018

Danny has this really great life mission. It's to raise our boys to be productive members of society and make sure they are better off than we are. I think that's a beautiful mission and that drives him. I don't feel like I have a life mission. I don't know what drives me. And that *makes me sad. I feel stuck. I know I have the power to make a change, but I'm scared. Fear is preventing me from doing something else. I just applied for a new job back in tech for Head of Americas. It's more pay, more work, and a longer commute. As if any of that would somehow make me happier. But that's what I do. I just bury myself deeper and deeper. Buy a Benz. Get stuck in corporate America. I did it on purpose but now I want to leave more than ever. My boss is coming from the UK next week. Will I have the guts to just quit? Probably not, but I sure wish I did.*

There's a lot to unpack in this short excerpt, but five key points stand out:

1. Through this journal entry, I gained insight into the fact that lacking a life mission marked a critical source of negative emotion for me. Its absence was a source of sadness and created a feeling of being stuck. If we don't actively have a mission, how can we know where we're going?

2. I had fears that needed to be worked through. After reviewing this, I realized I needed to write another journal entry on exactly what fears I perceived as a threat to making a change. Some may have been valid and real, though they could have been

mitigated with proper planning, while others might have been avoidable—all in my head and even silly.

3. I knew money, a better title, and more responsibility were not going to make me happy. My next question should have been, *If that doesn't make me happy, what will?*

4. My self-sabotaging behavior was to make things worse and harder for myself, to push myself further down the corporate path by applying for jobs I didn't really want. Another journal entry to explore why I felt the need to do that would've been a good idea.

5. I knew, for more than a year before I was laid off, that corporate culture was no longer for me. I was delaying stepping into my purpose out of the fear of causing myself more pain—pain that could have been avoided if I had just listened to myself and quit right then and there.

I hope this has been a helpful look at a real journal entry so you can apply the same scrutiny to your own journaling practice. If you already journal regularly, look at some of your past entries and see what you can decode. Writing your thoughts and feelings in a journal is the first step, but without going further, you'll miss the key insights. Reread your entries several times and reflect on what you wrote. Do you believe it? Is what you've written a valid thought with concrete evidence to back it up? Why do you feel that way? How could you change your perceptions? What actions could you take to feel differently? These are just a few things to consider.

By way of journaling, you're able to uncover limiting beliefs that hold you back, fears you've never articulated, and to dream big. Again, the key is not to self-edit. Just allow your thoughts to flow freely on the paper. If you don't journal regularly but would like to, here are some prompts to get you started:

- I feel most powerful when I'm…
- My biggest strengths are…
- If money and time and schooling weren't issues, what I'd really like to do for work is…
- My biggest supporters are…
- I've always dreamed of…
- A few careers I'd be interested in exploring are…

Meditation

Meditation is another great way to help you turn inward because you are training yourself to be in tune with your body, thoughts, and feelings. You may not gain insight during meditation itself, but as you cultivate a meditation practice, you may notice you improve your mental reflexes when it comes to knowing yourself and observing the world around you. If you're new to meditation, it doesn't have to be an intimidating practice. Here are some steps to follow as you get started:

1. Start by sitting in a chair, legs uncrossed in front of you, feet firmly on the ground. Lay your palms flat on your thighs.
2. Breathe in through your nose for a count of four.
3. Exhale through your mouth for a count of four.
4. Repeat this step several times, for about a minute, clearing your thoughts as they pop up so that you are only focused on your breath.
5. Then add in a short mantra. On the inhale, think, *I am open to my innermost thoughts and feelings.* On the exhale, think, *I release all blockers that are holding me back.*

Stay in this meditative space for at least five minutes. The longer you can hold your focus during your meditation practice, the more comfortable you'll become with turning inward.

Intuition: Going Beyond Practical Tools

Journaling and meditation are great ways to more readily turn inward when you need to, but sometimes we just have to rely on good ol' intuition, as well as trial and error. Initially, after leaving corporate life, I thought I might want to be a health coach. I took a few classes, spoke with a few health coaches, and even interviewed with a company that offered health coaching certifications. After much inward reflection, I realized helping women with their health alone wasn't exactly what I wanted, but in that process I learned about life coaching! You never know what your exploration may yield. The more open to possibility that you are, the sooner you'll find your calling.

Not to worry if one strategy to finding internal fulfillment doesn't work; there are several ways to begin the process of turning inward. I encourage you to try them all so you can figure out which suits you best. It's kind of like clothes shopping. Sometimes the shirt that looks the best on the hanger fits terribly, while the one shirt you thought you'd hate looks amazing. These exercises can sometimes look like they won't work, but in the end they might be the exact thing you needed to crack the surface and go deep.

Ultimately, the benefits of turning inward and discovering your purpose can contribute to getting unstuck, which will lead to a greater overall sense of well-being and happiness. When you're living a life that feels aligned with your values and goals, you'll experience a deeper sense of fulfillment and satisfaction, and be able to tackle the challenges and obstacles that come your way with greater ease and grace. Now that you've turned inward, you've set yourself on a path toward fulfilling your purpose and living a life that feels aligned and meaningful.

• •

Make It Happen

Get Creative

There are more ways than one to turn inward! Beyond journaling and meditation, you might consider engaging in creative activities like drawing, painting, or crafting to help stimulate the right side of the brain and increase intuition. Here are a few things you could try to get the juices flowing:

- Order a fun, new coloring book and break out a fresh set of colored pencils

- Take a painting class with a friend

- Sit in nature and sketch the wilderness

- Write a poem about something that inspires you

- Decorate a gift basket and give it to someone special

- Listen to a new song or piece of music and think about what it's saying to you

- Try cooking a new recipe with a loved one

Chapter 5

Rekindle Your Passions

Hobby means doing something for the fun
of it, not necessarily to make a living.

—THERESA A. HUSARIK, *HOBBY FARMING FOR DUMMIES*

We all had hobbies once upon a time. Perhaps as a kid you loved to draw, play school, dance, play an instrument, ride bikes with the neighborhood kids, or collect bugs. Over time, these hobbies were likely replaced with adult responsibilities: working, paying bills, cleaning your house, taking care of your pets, raising children, washing your car, and a host of other adulting activities. Lucky you! Of course you take pride and joy in these things, but day in and day out, the routine can leave you in the doldrums, especially when it's a thankless task like scrubbing the grout or when you haven't had a chance to do something for yourself in ages. You've heard me describe this as Groundhog Day before—the same thing playing out day after day.

As a result, we often forget about our passions and personal aspirations, which leaves us feeling unfulfilled and disconnected from our true selves. But you don't have to settle for this lifestyle. You can take a hint from your former self and spice things up a bit. I know, I know, you're uber-busy and don't have time to spice *anything* up, right? And what hobby would you even want to pick up these days? You probably wouldn't be any good, huh?

I'm sorry, but that's 100 percent BS. Yes, I just called BS on you. But I mean it with love, so don't get offended.

If it makes you feel better, I had to call BS on myself back in 2017. I secretly missed dancing *so much*. It had been years since I'd taken a hip-hop class and even longer since I'd taken ballet. The occasional pirouette in my kitchen while making dinner didn't really count. I was a dance major in college, so it's a wonder I let eight years pass me by without dancing formally. Even so, I can relate to the protestations you're putting up: work was my priority, leaving little time for anything in the pleasure, fun, or recreation category.

In a rare move after my Vegas trip, when I saw the Jabbawockeez perform live, I decided to take a week off from work to determine if I wanted to quit and be a stay-at-home mom, find a new job, or suck it up and continue with my life as it was. I should note that this was a year prior to the journal entry you read in the previous chapter. Talk about not seeing the signs or being honest with myself!

I worked up the courage to attend a popping class at Broadway Dance Center in the city, and since I'd paid for the bus fare in, I figured I might as well eat lunch at the studio and stay for the Floor-Barre class afterward. There I was, stretching out ahead of class in a pair of sweatpants, a sports bra, the coolest hooded zip-up shirt I could find in my closet, and a pair of dirty old sneakers. No doubt I felt old and out of place, but I was there, and that was something to celebrate. I felt a mixture of anxiety and exhilaration that I hadn't felt in years. While everyone else was at work, making PowerPoints and hoping that the operations review would be cancelled, I was about to spend my day living my passion. I wore a smile that spread from ear to ear.

Of course, I struggled with my stamina in a ninety-minute popping class. The dance genre has its roots in hip-hop but was totally different from the styles I'd studied. I was rusty for sure, but I did reasonably well considering how long it had been since my last class. Dance was now my hobby, and as Theresa Husarik said in the epigraph to this chapter, that meant this class was all about fun for me. There was zero pressure to turn my dancing experience into a revenue stream or to go professional. And thank God for that! The entire day was a reality check. Fourteen minutes into the Floor-Barre class, I caught my second wind. I was feeling like a boss and settling into studio life again…but twenty-eight minutes in, I was hoping the teacher would be hit with a case of diarrhea so class would end early! My legs were stricken with cramps. I could barely keep from writhing in charley-horse-induced pain on the floor, while everyone else was in a delicate developpé.

I made it through both classes, though, and I limped out, feeling accomplished. My heart was beaming with the most beautiful feeling. I had unlocked a piece of my former self, a self I could no longer ignore. And why would I want to? I deserved to feed my soul, which I had neglected for far too long. I needed an outlet beyond my daily workout routine. I needed dance, self-expression, and freedom of movement. The confines of corporate America were wearing me down, but dance was putting me back together in an even more magnificent way. I couldn't wait to figure out the next time I could plan an escape to Manhattan for a dance class. It kept me going during the adulting doldrums. It gave me something I hadn't felt in a long time, something I thought was gone for good. It gave me *hope*—hope for a better life, a happier life, a more fulfilling life; hope that maybe I hadn't made my bed, which I now had to lie in forever. Rather, I could make a new bed, a comfier bed that I'd actually be excited to jump into.

In the sections that follow, let's explore why hobbies are more than just a fun way to fill your time; how to return to the hobbies of your youth (or even try a new one on for size); and wrap up with the only two reasons I can think of that should *not* drive your motivation to take up a hobby.

Why Hobbies Are Important

Research has shown that having a hobby has many benefits, from improved health and well-being to professional growth. A hobby can be a very welcome mental break, especially for type A personalities who struggle to unplug from work. A hobby that is more physical in nature will help you stay in shape. Ballroom dancing, for instance, has been recommended to seniors to help with posture and boosting blood circulation, so you might as well get a head start on that now.

Speaking of getting older, one other thing to remember is that your life probably won't always be this busy with work and kids and so on. Someday down the road you'll retire, your children will move out, and then what will you fill your time with? If you have no hobbies outside of your roles as a professional and/or a parent, you may find unnecessary anxiety leading up to that point. You may even experience a midlife or identity crisis as you try to figure out who you are as you navigate these life changes. You can futureproof your well-being by getting a jump on your hobbies now.

If you're especially type A and goal-oriented, I imagine you're asking yourself how rediscovering a childhood hobby is going to help you at all when it comes to grabbing life by your dreams. *How is nine years of youth orchestra going to help me launch my business or rekindle a connection with my partner, Karin?!* you might be wondering.

Though rediscovering old hobbies may not directly impact your goals, one very crucial reason to do it all the same is that *you can't fill someone else's cup when you're scraping the bottom of your own well.*

I'll say it again for the people in the back: *When you haven't done anything for yourself in a long time, isn't it harder to show up for others in your life? Isn't it harder to show up for Future You?* This is especially important to digest for anyone who works full time (and then some!) or who is a loved one's caregiver, as burnout can crop up very quickly. Making time in your schedule to do something fun and entirely for yourself is critical.

If you still need help convincing yourself that taking up a hobby will be a worthwhile use of your time, here are six strong reasons to get you started. Hobbies and interests can:

1. **Improve Mental Health.** Engaging in an activity that you are passionate about can reduce stress and anxiety because it provides a sense of escape and relaxation. Additionally, it can increase happiness, which in turn enhances overall mental health.

2. **Provide a Sense of Purpose.** Having a passion gives women purposefulness, direction, and meaning in their lives, helping us to feel more fulfilled and satisfied. When you are more fulfilled and satisfied, you're naturally going to be happier. Plus, it helps us to feel accomplished, which strengthens our understanding of our purpose.

3. **Increase Confidence and Self-Esteem.** Pursuing passions and achieving goals can help women

feel more confident and prouder of themselves, which in turn boosts their self-esteem and sense of worth. We'll dive into confidence more deeply in Chapter 8, since this is one of the most important skills to master.

4. **Foster Creativity.** Engaging in creative pursuits such as writing, painting, or photography can stimulate the imagination and help women tap into their innate creative abilities. A study published in *Psychology of Aesthetics, Creativity, and the Arts* states that "mind-wandering" activities that require a moderate level of focus can even help generate creative ideas and solutions we may not reach if we force ourselves to stay at our desks and focus directly on a problem. Not to mention this also helps you deepen your intuition as you did while turning inward. I'm sure you can see how all of these steps feed into each other.

5. **Promote Personal Growth.** Pursuing passions allows women to learn new skills, challenge themselves, and grow as individuals. This can lead to greater self-awareness, personal insight, and a deeper sense of fulfillment.

6. **Develop Social Connections.** Joining a recreational league or craft circle can bring new friends into your life, something that we know is difficult to do as an adult. One of my clients met her best friend, who officiated her wedding, because

she signed up for a poetry workshop she'd always wanted to try. Additionally, you may meet your next boss or business partner, or get a new donor for a campaign you're running. The possibilities are endless, but only if you take the action to get involved in a hobby.

Beyond all this, according to an article in *Antioxidants & Redox Signaling*, one of the main reasons why hobbies are important is that they can provide the benefits of doing group activities, which could help you overcome any sense of loneliness you may be experiencing. Social isolation and even the perception of social isolation (loneliness) are associated with a higher risk of mortality because they're both risk factors for cardiovascular disease; this is because lonely individuals have increased peripheral vascular resistance and elevated blood pressure. We were made to experience connection with others, and a hobby will help you do just that, while keeping your heart healthy at the same time.

Another study's findings in the *Journal of Epidemiology* in 2016 suggested that having no hobbies may be more strongly linked to the risk of mortality and functional decline than lacking a purpose in life. Whoa—read that again! Having a hobby may be more beneficial to your health than having a defined purpose in life!

Don't worry; I'm not going to stat you to death. Hopefully you get the picture: having hobbies leads to a happier, healthier, more fulfilling life.

How to Return to Hobbies of Your Youth

Think about what you enjoyed doing as a kid. Is there a way you can rediscover that passion as an adult? If so, that's great! Many cities and towns have parks departments, recreational leagues, civic bands or orchestras, and clubs you can look into and join.

Realistically, some hobbies might not be as feasible as we age. For example, if you played rugby in college, that might be tough to continue at fifty years old, but it doesn't mean you can't still be in proximity of your hobby. You could watch a local match or coach a team in your spare time. You might even find a lower-impact sport similar to rugby, like soccer or flag football. Get creative and dare to be different. Maybe you want to start a youth league to expose children to the game? Or start a fantasy league?

There are so many ways to stay involved with the things you're passionate about. A friend I used to dance with got a job at Capezio, one of the nation's leading dancewear companies. Even though she was no longer dancing herself, she was able to stay involved in her passion. One of my friends who also grew up dancing, though at a lower level, initially enrolled in adult ballet classes to rediscover her hobby, but whenever she was in class, all she could focus on was how much stamina and flexibility she'd lost. It was demoralizing, and for a while, she stopped going. Soon after, though, she enrolled in a Pilates studio, where the classes work a lot of the same muscles as a dance class. She says it's exciting to put those skills to use and to feel like she's learning something new at the same time!

Discovering New Hobbies and Interests

On the other hand, maybe you don't have the desire to resume an old hobby. If so, it may be time to break new ground, try something totally different. It's perfectly normal not to want to go back to an old passion, especially if it was something your parents pushed you into or that you competed in at a very high level. You may have been burnt-out or harbor bad feelings toward it. You now have an opportunity to pick something you would love to try.

Remember, not every hobby has to be musical or sporty in nature. Gardening, crocheting, hiking, joining a book club, playing cards, or attending Bible study all come to mind as potential hobbies you could explore.

Not sure which hobby to take up? You know me and my journaling! The best way to get started is by answering one or more of the following prompts:

- When I was a child, an activity I enjoyed was _____, because _____.
- I always wanted to learn…
- If time and money weren't an issue, I'd take up _____ hobby.
- I'm happiest when I'm doing _____.
- Friends and family tell me I'm really talented at _____.
- How could a new hobby help me in my professional life?

You might also find a new hobby by asking friends and family what hobbies they enjoy; in doing so, you may find something that piques your interest. I know I told you earlier to turn inward. But this is once instance where some outward exploration might serve you. That doesn't mean you're going to immediately sign up for whatever hobby they love. Once you have a list from others, you can turn inward and evaluate which of these, if any, you'd enjoy exploring. Or you could do a Google search on the best hobbies in your area or for your skill set. I did a search on "best hobbies for former dancers" and came up with lots of interesting options. You might even check your local coffee shop's bulletin board for flyers and activity listings or the Meetup app to connect with other people in your area with similar interests. And, of course, don't forget to look for signs from the Universe. You never know how you might be guided to your next big breakthrough.

The specific hobby you choose doesn't matter as long as you enjoy it. Let's spend a minute on the concept of enjoyment for enjoyment's sake, though, because somewhere along the line there was an imaginary memo that went out to all, which said: *You have to be good at your hobby. It should be easy and you should never feel any growing pains or discomfort in your hobby.*

Once again, I call BS on that notion. Sometimes a new hobby is a challenge, but that doesn't mean it isn't a great hobby. Take learning to play the guitar, for instance. Unless you're a prodigy and somehow pick it up lickety-split, you're going to struggle with hitting the right chords, getting your fingers in the right position, and, if you're small like me, just holding the guitar in your arms will be a major feat. But that's no reason not to give it a shot anyway!

Finally, don't worry if you get your hobby "wrong." It isn't the end of the world if you pick a bad fit on your first try. This is all about exploration, so try a few hobbies until you find what sticks and brings you joy. If you're not having fun, keep looking for a new hobby. Just don't get having fun and being good at something confused. As I mentioned, any new hobby will take some time to perfect. That can even be part of the fun!

Practical Considerations for Your New (or Old!) Hobby

There are other considerations you should keep in mind when selecting a hobby, such as your budget. Yacht racing might seem like a really cool hobby that you'd enjoy, but if you don't have a yacht or the budget to buy one and pay a crew, then this might not be a good fit after all. You'll also want to consider the style of your personality. Are you competitive by nature? If not, a hobby that involves competing against others will probably create more frustration than peace in your life. Do your research and try a few out. You might surprise yourself with what you find you enjoy.

If you're reading this and thinking, *That's great, but how will I ever fit this into my busy schedule?* it sounds like you need to start by examining your priorities. (Here comes the tough love again.) We make time for what we deem important. How many people have a favorite Netflix series that they somehow magically carve out time to binge-watch or to attend a watch party on release night? You may even be carving out time unconsciously, such as when my husband and I realized we were frittering away our weeknights by watching the news. With this in mind, what if you started consciously carving out time in your calendar for your hobby? If you set aside dedicated time, you'll be far more likely to follow through on rekindling your passions and rediscovering joy in your busy life.

As with most things, I'd advise you start small. Instead of signing up for tennis, cycling, *and* the gardening club all at once, pick one hobby to start. Then add it into your calendar on a monthly or biweekly basis until you can work up to the level of participation that works for you. You don't necessarily need a weekly hobby, but you could have one if you wanted to.

When I started taking in-person dance classes, I knew once a month was about all I was willing to fit into my schedule, given the commute from New Jersey to New York and the need to arrange for childcare. Weekends were perfect because my husband was off from work. But when I started doing online yoga classes, too, I knew I could easily fit them in two mornings a week, before the kids woke up.

Perhaps you have a seasonal hobby that will keep you busier at a specific time of year. If you love snowboarding, that might not require much of your time between May and August, but in the winter months you'll likely be taking more trips to find the best powder. Let those around you know your love for the hobby and, if needed, how enjoying that hobby benefits your life. While I don't suggest asking for permission to engage in your hobby, there is a certain level of communication that will be needed to maintain healthy relationships when your hobby's season is at its peak. For instance, I wouldn't expect my husband to be super supportive if I told him, "I'm leaving for three weeks to go snowboarding; good luck managing the household." A weekend trip with the girls, on the other hand, would be a nonissue. Similarly, your bestie might not be happy about you taking off to the Caribbean for the summer to go scuba diving, scuppering any plans you'd made or could have made with her, but if she's a true friend she'll understand when you explain your hobby's importance.

Eventually, your hobby will become an everyday part of your life. A habit, if you will. But that doesn't mean you don't have to be diligent about scheduling it in your calendar and honoring the promises you've made to yourself by following through with its importance. Especially as you're building your hobby back into your routine, be conscientious that you don't cancel on yourself because something that other people *want* (but don't need) you to do has cropped up.

Two Reasons NOT to Adopt a Hobby

As a type A person myself, I know the impulse to try to get multiple uses out of a new hobby. In a way, it allays the guilt you might feel for doing something "selfish." Below are two related reasons I don't think you should let fuel your decision to adopt a hobby. By the end of this section, I hope you'll understand the difference between self*ish* and self-*interested*, and that it will have hit home that you are doing nothing wrong by taking a little time for yourself on a regular basis.

DON'T Take Up a Hobby Solely to Turn It into a "Side Hustle."

The #GirlBoss culture of the 2010s morphed into something even more insidious during the pandemic. Stuck at home, a lot of us turned to bread baking and crafting for comfort and something to while away all our new downtime, but as COVID restrictions started to lift, it felt like everyone and their mother had turned their hobbies into a hustle, to the point that you get it from every side. Well-meaning people will say, "Hey, you could make money selling these!" as though there's no other reason you would have taken up jewelry making or cross-stitch, and while they might be right, this can also become another source of stress, not stress relief!

It's fine to want to earn extra income from a hobby, but if you turn inward, as you did in Chapter 4, and feel stressed out at the prospect of, say, researching how to sell at markets, please know that it's okay to have creative play and impractical hobbies—that is, ones that aren't making a quick buck—in adult life. It's a key way to unwind and tune in.

DON'T Force Your Hobby into Date Night or "Mommy and Me" Bonding.

Sometimes guilt over taking up a hobby isn't extrinsic, but rather self-fueled. You might feel guilty doing something for yourself, so you instead ask your partner to join you for a night of rock climbing as a "fun date night." It's not their cup of tea, so you go twice and then never go again. While it was well-intended, don't stress if it didn't work out. You and your partner don't have to share all the same hobbies. They can support you from the sidelines. This is a part of your week that is *all for you*. It is going to feel scary and selfish to carve out this time, but you're doing things for other people constantly. Selfish and self-interested are not the same, girlfriend! You deserve this time.

However, if you feel the urge to include your partner or your kids in your hobby and they do enjoy it, go for it! Why not make it a twofer? Now that my son is older and runs cross-country, we're able to fit in runs together and get some extra bonding time. With that said, if I started running *only* so we could hang out and then he didn't want to one day, I'd be pretty bummed. The fact is, I love running either way. Having him along for the ride is a bonus.

If you have little ones at home and it breaks your heart to hear them say, "Why is Mommy going out again?" when you've just laced up your running shoes, recruit your partner or co-parent to help explain that you do a lot for your family, and this is something that you do to make sure you can always care for them. Explaining to even young children the impor- tance of taking time to recharge and turn inward is actually setting a fantastic example for your kids. It is one I hope they will thank you for later in life when they are courageous enough to set boundaries and take time for their health and well-being too. And for all the single moms out there, you know the saying *It takes a village*. Don't be afraid to ask for help. Enlist a friend to watch your children or look for hobbies at places that offer childcare.

In today's fast-paced world, women find themselves juggling multiple roles and responsibilities, from being a mother and a wife to holding down a job and taking care of the household. But with a little planning and focus, you can open space in your week for fun, creativity, and rekindling your passions. It's never too late to start, and the rewards are well worth the effort. By embracing your passions and pursuing your goals, you can lead a happier, more fulfilling life and set a positive example for others.

• •

Make It Happen

Hobby Hopping

Still unsure which hobby you'll choose? Why not take a few months to explore several new hobbies or interests and see which one(s) you enjoy most? Take a pickleball class at the country club, learn to make pottery at the local arts college, or go for an early morning swim at the YMCA.

Start a log of your hobby experiences. The activity can take place weekly or monthly depending on how often you're willing and able to engage in it, but try not to go longer than a month without engaging in your chosen hobby or trying out a new one. You can use the space to the right or track your experience in your own journal, preferred notes app, or on a separate piece of paper.

If you're part of my Facebook group, Successful Working Women Rocking Reinvention, I encourage you to post a picture of yourself doing your hobby so that we can celebrate you! Use the hashtag #FillYourOwnCup in your post and be sure to celebrate someone else's hobby adventure while you're there.

Hobby	Date	What I enjoyed about this experience	What I didn't enjoy or could improve

Chapter 6

Let's Get Spiritual

Faith sees the invisible, believes the
unbelievable, and receives the impossible.

—CORRIE TEN BOOM, *JESUS IS VICTOR*

One Thursday evening, I stared down the highway ahead of me. There was nothing but red brake lights for miles. *Awesome*, I thought sarcastically. *Another night of missing dinner with my kids.*

I unzipped my lunch bag and pulled out an apple to hold me over till I got home. I had learned to pack extra food for my long commute.

"My Name is Jonas" by Weezer blasted from my car's Bluetooth speakers. I couldn't help but laugh at how much that song mimicked my life in the corporate world. I was longing to do something more creative. These guys got to live their dream and sing for a living; meanwhile, I was suffocating in my job, feeling completely burnt out. *How is that fair?* I wondered.

As my Benz inched forward, melancholy song after melancholy song rang through my speakers. The Smashing Pumpkins' "Disarm" and Puddle of Mudd's "Blurry" were on heavy rotation. It was almost as if I enjoyed the sulking, helpless feeling they created in me. Suddenly a thought popped into my head, something that had never occurred to me.

Am I making myself sad on purpose? Do I somehow enjoy this toxic feeling?

I didn't want to answer myself because I knew that was exactly what I was doing.

What if I listened to more upbeat music? I posited. *Would my mood actually change with it?*

Bingo! I was filling my head with melancholy music to match my mood, which in turn reinforced my mood to match the music. It was a vicious cycle, and I was the one perpetuating it. I let it happen night after night.

Instinctively my hand turned off my phone's music and flipped on the radio. I hit the scan button and stumbled on a new station as I aggressively jockeyed between cars on I-95.

The song had a vaguely familiar hip-hop feeling, but the lyrics were of peace and love. The station that lifted my spirituality fog? K-Love.

I know that, for a few readers, a warning bell went off in your heads when you read the name of the popular Christian contemporary music station K-Love. It has taken me a hella long time to admit I like country music, and it's taken me even longer to confess my love for Christian rock. Obviously I was worried about how others would react, but as I've come to learn, I'm the one living my life, not others, and since my tastes aren't hurting anyone, it shouldn't matter what they think of me or my choices.

Some of you may still be thinking, *Be that as it may, I don't appreciate you pushing your religious views on me.*

I hear you loud and clear. It is never my intention to proselytize to a reader or a client. As a life coach, my goal is to create a judgment-free zone where all my clients can show up and authentically be themselves. I've coached atheists, Christians, Jews, and women who were in touch with the spirit world, to name a few, and I've never once pushed my beliefs on their situations. In fact, a good, seasoned life coach is trained *not* to let their values interfere with their clients' beliefs. If you're considering hiring one, I think your decision regarding sharing a religious background with your chosen coach can come down to personal preference.

Whether or not we have the same faith, in this book's introduction, I promised to share *all* the secrets that allowed me to transform my life, so it's only right that I include this instrumental piece of the puzzle: faith and spirituality.

Can you reinvent your life without giving any consideration to spiritual beliefs? Absolutely.

Do I believe my life is better because I took the time to consider my beliefs and deepen my faith? Yes, 100 percent.

Now, let's make like Steven Curtis Chapman and dive in deep.

Examining and Reconnecting to My Own Beliefs

As a kid, I never questioned my beliefs to any real extent. I was born and baptized Episcopalian, a Protestant denomination of Christianity. Every Sunday morning we went to church, no questions asked. We stayed until the last note on the organ was played, and then we lived the rest of the week like any other decent, moral people. Since my dad ran the acolyte, or altar server, program, I became an acolyte as well, though I didn't understand the significance. Other than that, we celebrated the big holidays, took communion, and went to Sunday school. Pretty standard practices.

When I went off to college, as many of us do, I forgot all about church. None of my friends went, and most mornings I was flat-out too hungover to attend. (I did still pray a lot, mostly to thank God for getting me through the drunken mess I had been the night before. Let's be honest: if you've ever drunk more than your body could handle, you've probably resorted to praying while huddled over a toilet, hurling your guts out.)

I dropped in and out of church after college, though I always seemed to be drawn back to my religious roots for one reason or another. I still prayed, sometimes to ask Him to help me land a job or, later in life, to care for my unborn baby.

My husband is Catholic, so after our kids were old enough to attend church with us, we began attending Mass more regularly and enrolled them in Catholic school. Once we moved to South Carolina, I felt called to deepen my religious practice even further by attending women's Bible study in addition to regular Sunday services.

Even so, I still had my fears and hang-ups, including, as you may recall from Chapter 1, a strong fear of death and dying. When I confided in my husband about the 3 a.m. panic attacks I'd been having, he was shocked and eager to help. He thought because I believed in God, I must not fear death, and yet I did. A lot!

It wasn't until he gave me a copy of Kelvin Chin's book *Overcoming the Fear of Death* that I inspected my beliefs a bit more closely, beyond the surface level of believing in God because I'd always believed in God. Chin explains that you cannot logically believe in Heaven and be scared of dying at the same time. If you need to read that again, I don't blame you. I felt the same way. Mr. Chin was lovingly calling BS on me, and he was right. Either I didn't really believe in my religion or I was temporarily going insane, but it couldn't be both. Why was I really so scared of dying? What about death had me rocked to my core, paralyzed with fear?

Through a lot of journaling, I came to an answer. I was afraid I was wasting my life. My job was making me miserable, and every day felt like a chore. That was no way to live. I knew this couldn't have been why God put me here. My sperm of all sperms did not fertilize that egg so I could make PowerPoint presentations to justify my existence to a bunch of assholes. (Did I just swear in the spiritual chapter? Well, it's how I felt at the time.) There had to be more to life.

Maybe I'm not scared of dying because I don't know where I'd end up, I thought. *Maybe, instead, it's about wasting the one life God has given me. Maybe I wouldn't be so scared of dying if I was actually living my purpose and reaching my full potential. Who has my Creator made me to be? Do I have the courage and faith to find out?* Turns out, it wasn't so much that I was afraid of dying, because I really did believe in a heavenly afterlife. The bigger issue was that I wasn't living in full alignment with my beliefs. The point is, this was a liberating moment for me. I was now in a place where I had consciously aligned with my beliefs. Armed with these insights, I could now make the necessary changes. It was time for me to put my faith to the test.

Examining and Reconnecting to Your Belief System

Have you ever stopped to really explore your beliefs?

We all have a belief system, which is shaped by our experiences. If you were raised by people who kept all their money under a mattress, then I can see why you might believe banks are evil. On the flip side, if your parents worked in finance, then you probably trust the banks and keep the majority of your investments with financial institutions.

The same can be said for spirituality. We are likely to either hold the beliefs our parents gave us or to have changed our outlook based on experience and external influences that have persuaded us in some compelling way. The problem is most of us get caught up in the daily grind and take our beliefs for granted or follow generational beliefs that we thought would serve us only to find they led us down the wrong path. When is the last time you questioned your beliefs or stopped to think if you believe them with your whole heart? For our purposes, I'm now inviting you to deeply examine, or reexamine, your beliefs and set your life in alignment with *your* beliefs. It's time to sort through your belief system and determine what stays, what goes, and what other information you need to reframe your life. How can you embark on this process? For starters, self-reflection is a good place to begin.

If you'd like to examine your beliefs, including whether you're living your life in alignment with them, get out your journal and answer the following questions:

1. What was my relationship with religion and spirituality growing up? In what faith or faiths did my parents raise me, if any? Did I attend

our place of worship because I was made to or
because I wanted to?

2. How has my relationship with faith changed
since childhood and adolescence? Is it the same?
Different? What impacted that change?

3. Are my thoughts, decisions, and actions today
made in alignment with what I say I believe? In
other words, am I talking the talk *and* walking
the walk? If not, what is one thing I can do this
week to change them to be more positive and
spiritually based?

Don't forget to listen for signs that may be drawing you in
a particular direction. They could be physical signs, like seeing
a poster about a church gathering, or somatic signs, like an
emptiness that needs to be filled. No matter how far I got from
church, I was always called back for one reason or another.
My soul needed it. What does your soul need?

Further, you may explore reading and researching beliefs
to get a deeper understanding or fill in the gaps that you
identified were missing. If you're comfortable opening up
to someone, as I eventually did with my husband, you may
consider talking to others about your beliefs and uncovering
how they see the world. Hearing another's perspective can help
broaden your understanding and help you find a community
of like-minded (or maybe even not-so-like-minded) individuals to join.

The Benefits of Connecting or Reconnecting to Your Spirituality

My newfound connection to my faith offered me additional benefits to the usual ones religion promises you, ones I hadn't anticipated.

Whether reconnecting with your spiritual side means going back to church, meditating or praying more, or even discovering for the first time the belief system that works for you, I hope undertaking this journey means you'll experience some of the same benefits I did.

Rewiring Your Brain

We already discussed how I used rewiring my brain to overcome my panic attacks, but I left out one critical part of that process.

During my quest to explore my relationship with death, I listened to the audiobook of *90 Minutes in Heaven*. As I heard Don Piper recount his experience, I couldn't help but think what a beautiful experience going to Heaven would one day be. It dawned on me that I could apply this thinking in the dark of night. I could train my brain to be excited about going there someday. Don't get me wrong; I was in no rush to kick the bucket, but it gave me a clear image to hope for when I did depart this world for the next. It was far more comforting than the black nothingness I had once envisioned. Without my faith, I wouldn't have had this opportunity to rewire my brain and change my relationship with my inevitable death.

Beyond its ability to help us cope with our own mortality, spirituality can help us reframe our thoughts in a more positive direction, as my experience listening to K-Love attests. When I'm having a bad day or I've made an error that I'm beating myself up over, I'm reminded that it's not the end of the world, I'm more than my mistakes, and there's so much good in the world. I can get in the car, hear one song, and my entire day gets turned around. It's my daily reminder that God's creation is far bigger than me. That notion helps remove a lot of the pressure I used to place on myself to be "successful" or impress others. I'm already loved by my Higher Power just the way I am.

What's more, engaging in activities like going to religious services, meditating, or reading your faith's holy texts can help to build a regular period of reflection into your schedule. By taking time to think about all that has been going on in your day-to-day life at regular intervals, like Sunday mornings, you can train your brain to be proactive rather than reactive to all the Universe throws at you.

Healing and Forgiveness

As I started reading books by religious authors, I realized I had built up work-related resentment that needed to be released if I had any hopes of getting unstuck. In Matthew Kelly's book *Life is Messy*, he says, "You are not what happened to you. You are not what you have accomplished. You are not even who you are today or who you have become so far. You are also who and what you are still capable of becoming. You are your realized and unrealized potential. God sees you and all your potential, and he aches to see you embrace your best, truest, highest self.… Allow the past to serve you. Don't let it rob you of your now. Don't let it steal your future."

Years of toxic workplace environments and negative comments from bosses, peers, and others were clouding my mind. I often replayed conversations in my head, wondering if I would be in a better situation if I had done something differently. But none of that mattered. I couldn't go back and change the past. How I had been treated wasn't right or fair, but the resulting anger and bitterness were poisoning me, stealing precious energy that I needed to reinvent my life.

Through the help of scripture, I was able to forgive those who mistreated me, even going so far as to pray for them in the process. I don't believe their actions were ever personal. It was merely fear that drove them to act the way they did: fear for their own job security, fear that they weren't living their own purpose, fear that they needed to be validated. Rather than be angry with them, I felt sympathy for them.

I wasn't who these people said I was. I used a daily affirmation to rewire my thoughts: *I am who God says I am.*

Who does your Higher Power say you are?

As you consider the answer to that question, here are some additional questions to ponder: Who do you need to forgive? What past events do you need to stop harping on? If the wounds are fresh, you may need some time to work through these emotions. A therapist or religious counselor could be a helpful place to start.

Overcoming Fear

In the book *Do Something Beautiful for God*—which, let's be real, I would not normally have picked up prior to my spiritual awakening—Mother Teresa motivated me in a way I hadn't felt before. She validated my fear and then gave me a loving kick in the pants to get me over it. I know it seems unlikely, but here's some of what she shared in her famous "Anyway" poem:

> "If you are successful you will win some false friends and true enemies; Succeed anyway."

> "What you spend years building someone could destroy overnight; Build anyway."

> "If you find serenity and happiness, they may be jealous; Be happy anyway."

I know you have some fears—we all do; take action anyway! The truth is God has a plan for your life, and it's up to you to take the steps to fully realize it. Knowing a Higher Power is in my corner, and in yours, too, provides a strength like no other.

Making Decisions

One of the most practical reasons for reconnecting with your spiritual beliefs is that you will become a better decision-maker. Your beliefs are a filter to run your decisions through, in addition to vetting the choices against your top goals.

Let's say your job promotes you but asks you to move across the country as a result. If you've determined what you believe on a spiritual level, you will then be able to look at your goals and your values holistically to help you make that decision. There isn't a right or wrong answer here, just the answer that works for you. One woman may choose to take the role because it will help her leave a legacy and contribute more to charity, while another woman of the same faith may decline the opportunity to stay local and care for her elderly parents. Same decision, different outcome based on not just their beliefs but also their individual values and goals.

It is worth noting, of course, that religion has historically been manipulated so that its tenets fit the rhetoric and needs of a powerful class of people, such as when women have stayed in abusive marriages because divorce is seen as sin or when antebellum Southern Christians used passages from the Bible to support the Atlantic slave trade. With this in mind, it is important that filtering your decisions through your beliefs doesn't mean giving into a religious "*should*." (Go back to Chapter 4 for a refresher on how bad the "shoulds" are!) Instead, it means that with prayer, a personal parsing of your holy text, and perhaps a private consultation with a trusted religious leader who shares your beliefs, you'll be better able to make *your* decisions.

Ask yourself some questions to discern the best direction for you at the present moment:

- What is my Higher Power guiding me to do?
- How do my options support or detract from my values?

     Will I be happy with this decision in three years? If not, what am I struggling with specifically?

Armed with your beliefs, you'll be able to make more solid decisions about your reinvention and create a life that is in harmony with your values.

Community and Connection

Your spiritual endeavors will surely expand your circle. As you make new friends and establish connections in your place of worship, you'll surround yourself with individuals who have similar goals and values. This newfound community can be a helpful source of motivation as you grab life by the dreams. These individuals may begin to play a bigger role in your reinvention, even challenging you in helpful ways. If you are starting a business, your new tribe may even appear among your first set of clients.

Happiness

This feels so simple as to be unquantifiable, but studies have shown that there is some correlation between being actively religious and having a happier outlook on life. In the US, according to Pew Research, 36 percent of the actively religious describe themselves as "very happy," compared with 25 percent of the inactively religious and 25 percent of the unaffiliated. What would change for you if you felt "very happy"? I'm willing to wager a lot.

Hope

Yep. I saved the biggest benefit for last. When all else fails, having a belief in something bigger than this world just might be the thing that pulls you through.

This world is full of crazy events that often leave us questioning our Higher Power. It's in these moments that our faith and hope in a bigger plan, far beyond our comprehension, can be a saving grace. No reinvention is without some level of struggle, but being able to have hope in a better future, one that you are intentionally designing, is both calming and freeing. Where are you putting your hope?

For me, answering those questions meant believing the Universe had my best interests at heart and that if I asked the Universe—or, in my case, God—for what I truly wanted, I would receive it. Seems like a no-brainer, right? If you take the appropriate steps to, let's say, get a new job in a new field that really interests you, you will be highly likely to achieve that goal. By thinking positive thoughts, asking your Higher Power for what you want, and taking the right steps, you are well on your way to success.

That said, if something doesn't work out the way you envisioned, a certain relinquishing of the outcome needs to happen. I'm not saying you should just give up, but you should become present to the signs you're receiving from the Universe and adjust course as needed. For example, when my first book, *The Ins and Outs of My Vagina*, wasn't an overnight hit, I could have taken that as a sign it wasn't meant to be. Or

I could have taken it as a sign that I needed to take a different marketing approach. I had to sit back and trust the path that God was making for me.

Maybe you've gotten through this chapter without tapping into your spiritual side. If that's you, and you're feeling a little down as a result of it, that's okay. For any number of reasons, from the traumatic to the mundane, perhaps you're not feeling especially spiritual or religious in this season of your life. Remember, I faced the same moments myself. Your needs may change with the seasons of life, so if this doesn't speak to you right now, it may down the road. Just know it will always be here for you if and when you want to tap into it.

This journey isn't over for me or you. It's one of constant growth and deeper understanding. I'm glad to be on this spiritual journey, and I invite you to start one of your own if you haven't already.

Make It Happen

I want to share some ways you can get in touch with your faith. The following are several religious and nonreligious ways to tap into your spirituality. Choose the ones that resonate with you. I can't wait to hear what happens!

Gratitude. We've talked about choosing gratitude before. Being grateful for all the gifts the Universe has bestowed on you, even when things seem to be going awry, is an act of bravery and faith. Intentional gratitude requires discipline to become fully engrained. It's a daily practice that takes consistent effort, but when it yields results, its bounty is amazing.

Feed your soul. What does your soul crave? It could be reading more or engaging in creative writing. You know when something is good for your soul—you may feel a deep warming inside or an indescribable elation. Hold on to those moments and examine what's causing them. Perhaps you're volunteering or giving back in some way. Seek to have more regular experiences that fill your soul in this way.

Trust your intuition. Intuition is a gift from your Higher Power. Learning to hear, trust, and follow your gut, or inner voice, can be a powerful way to engage your spiritual gifts. Tune in to your senses and explore the nagging signals from your mind and body.

Daily meditation. One of the most universal practices, meditation can be used to clear your mind and connect to your soul. Because meditation experiences are highly personal, they should never be rushed. Take your time and be present to whatever sensations or messages you receive.

Immersion in nature. You may find your inspiration and deepen your relationship with your soul by connecting to Mother Earth. As you soak up the beauty and flawless designs found in nature, you'll tap into your own beauty and purposeful design.

Listen to uplifting music. I fell in love with two Christian contemporary stations: K-Love and HIS Radio. They promised to have uplifting, positive music, and they delivered! I found myself enjoying my commutes and receiving messages I needed to hear to keep striving after my big goals. While listening to Christian music works for me, you could find music that meets your spiritual needs. Try listening to different styles of music for thirty days to see how it improves your life. There are lots of other stations to choose from on streaming services, such as spa music or classical music.

Study a religious text. Whatever your faith, it could be interesting to learn more about another faith and how it could apply to your life. While I chose a Bible study to deepen my understanding of Christian teachings, you might choose to study a different belief like Daoism, Judaism, or Buddhism. The study of a religious text can bring new insights and may even bring newfound friends to boot. Once I had other women in my network who could challenge me on my beliefs and help me grow deeper in my faith, I got stronger and more committed to my chosen way of life.

Volunteer. Pew Research found that, in the US, 58 percent of actively religious people are also involved in at least one nonreligious voluntary organization compared with just 51 percent of the inactively religious and 39 percent of the unaffiliated. You might volunteer at a local shelter or for a cause you're passionate about. It doesn't need to be spiritual in nature! I joined my local chapter of Junior League and was able to give back to the community in that way. From helping at our thrift shop to leading community conversations on the dangers of sex trafficking and prevalence of child abuse, I felt a bigger impact on the community and fed my soul. (By the way, we'll discuss volunteering in greater depth in Chapter 9!)

Take classes. Whether you're diving deeper into a religious faith or learning the art of meditation, it can be fruitful to learn from others who have been there, done that. Why not take a class to discover and explore your beliefs?

Chapter 7

Make Over Your Mindset

Many growth-minded people didn't even plan to go to the top. They got there as a result of doing what they love. It's ironic: The top is where the fixed-mindset people hunger to be, but it's where many growth-minded people arrive as a by-product of their enthusiasm for what they do.

—CAROL DWECK, *MINDSET: THE NEW PSYCHOLOGY OF SUCCESS*

The Drowning Man

There's an anecdote I've heard a handful of preachers give over the years. In it, a man is stuck on his rooftop during a flood and is praying to God for help.

Before he finishes saying, "Amen," a man in a rowboat comes by and yells, "Hey, jump in! I can take you to safety."

The stranded man waves him off. "No, that's all right! I'm praying to God, and he is going to save me."

So the rowboat goes on.

Then a motorboat comes by. The guy driving the motorboat shouts, "Jump in! I can save you."

To this the stranded man says, "No, thanks, I'm praying to God, and he is going to save me."

So the man in the motorboat shrugs and goes on.

The floodwaters are rising and looking grim, but still the man has faith. A helicopter comes by, and the pilot shouts down, "Grab this rope! I will lift you to safety."

To this the stranded man again replies, "No, thanks, I'm praying to God, and he is going to save me. I have faith."

So the helicopter reluctantly flies away.

Soon the water rises above the rooftop, and the man drowns. When he arrives in Heaven, he sees his opportunity to discuss this whole situation with God, at which point he exclaims, "I had faith in you, but you didn't save me. You let me drown! I don't understand why!"

To this God replies, "I sent you a rowboat and a motorboat and a helicopter. What more did you expect?"

Sometimes, to truly have a breakthrough, we need to stop being like the drowning man in the parable, waiting for some magical solution to our problems. If we sit around moping about our lives, ignoring the signs, or doing the same thing over and over expecting something to miraculously change, nothing will ever get better. As long as you're stuck in this negative perspective, you'll continue to attract more of the same. You might even make this victim story your whole identity.

If this sounds like you, you're not entirely to blame. You might be acting this way in response to positive external stimulation, such as if you have ever benefited from your victim mentality.

Put more simply, have you ever had someone dote on you for a week while you were sick or recovering from a medical procedure? At the time, you might have thought, *This is nice; I feel special.* Next thing you know, you're playing sick more often, using your ailments as a crutch to get the attention you seek but don't feel you can otherwise attain.

For another example, maybe you find yourself in toxic relationship after toxic relationship, but you find it difficult to leave because your problematic partners pay for all your expenses. You're not happy in your relationship, but that financial benefit is hard to pass up.

Or have you complained about needing to get back in shape, fully aware that you're doing nothing to fix the problem? You know, you still drink three sodas a day, never hit the gym, and won't touch a veggie, yet every time you see your besties, you complain about how out of shape you are. You're essentially saying, "I want you to know I acknowledge the problem, have no intention of doing anything about it, but please, keep feeling sorry for me."

This may sound harsh, but at some point, you either have to stop complaining or take steps to change your situation. How do you start? *By changing your mindset.* If you don't, this way of thinking will likely become part of your narrative—the overarching story of your life. Is that the story you really want to tell? Is that the life you want to live, always playing the victim? Letting your thoughts become deep-seated limiting beliefs that actually prevent you from making progress? I doubt it.

Choosing a Growth Mindset

So, what kind of thinking do you need to adopt to change your circumstances? A growth mindset, of course!

In no way, shape, or form will I attempt to improve upon what the talented American psychologist Carol Dweck has already identified in her work on mindset, but I want to give you an overview of her findings here. (If you're interested, you can find more information in her book *Mindset: The New Psychology of Success* or her TED Talk, "The Power of Yet.")

In 2006, Dweck discovered that people have two types of mindset: *fixed* or *growth*. Children who were praised for their efforts versus their innate abilities were more likely to develop a growth mindset, while children who were told they *were* good or bad at something tended to have a fixed mindset. Through her extensive research studies, particularly in early childhood development, Dweck found that a person's mentality isn't set in stone. In fact, we can hold a different mindset depending on the context or situation, so you might have a fixed mindset at work but a growth mindset in your personal relationships.

Essentially, someone with a *fixed mindset* believes that intelligence and talent are finite. You're born with what you got, and there's nothing you can do to change or improve that. A fixed mindset is usually the source of both limiting beliefs and the negative inner voice you hear. It results in statements such as "I can't," "I won't," and "I am not."

A person with a *growth mindset*, on the other hand, believes they can absolutely change and improve their talents and intelligence. They believe intelligence is flexible and adaptable and that you can grow your brain's capacity, not only to learn information and tasks, but to solve new problems—big problems. In a growth mindset your beliefs will sound like statements that start with "I can," "I will," and "I am." (Notice the positive construction here versus the negative construction of a fixed mindset. More on that later!)

You might be wondering why you should adopt a growth mindset. What makes it better than a fixed mindset? Don't we all reach a point of diminishing returns with our abilities, after all?

For starters, by preventing you from feeling that, hey, maybe middle management is all you're meant to attain, a growth mindset can lead to personal and professional growth, something most high-achieving women seek. It can also improve your resilience and enhance your problem-solving skills—two traits that are essential to both corporate and entrepreneurial careers. Beyond this, other people, such as your coworkers and friends, will gravitate to you when you display the positivity that comes along with a growth mindset.

Still need more reasons to adopt a growth mindset? Women with a growth mindset also possess the ability to adapt and cope with stressful or difficult situations, not to mention to recover quickly from setbacks. What would be possible for you if you developed a growth mindset? What might you accomplish? Whose life might you positively impact? Take some time to think about those questions and journal your responses. Your first step in all of this is to acknowledge that you *want* a growth mindset. Without that initial commitment, the rest of the steps will be a challenge at best.

Are you committed to a growth mindset? Yeah? Atta girl!

Identifying Our Own Blind Spots

Off the bat, you might be thinking, "I don't *need* to commit to a growth mindset. I definitely have a growth mindset *already*."

I mean, who would actually admit to having a fixed mindset? Not me! Yet if I look at so many of my past decisions, I can see I was actually operating with a fixed mindset.

In 2017, at the height of my midlife crisis, I felt that I couldn't leave my job. In a journal entry, I wrote, "I'm the breadwinner. How irresponsible would that be?" I didn't even think I could find another job that offered as much pay as my soul-crushing corporate one. (Hello, fixed mindset. *Hellooo*, limiting beliefs.)

No wonder I felt so stuck—I was resistant to any change! I couldn't fathom a world where I wasn't making six figures, paid by a global corporation.

Can you relate? Look back at the quotation from Carol Dweck that kicked off this chapter: *The top is where the fixed-mindset people hunger to be, but it's where many growth-minded people arrive as a by-product of their enthusiasm....* No wonder I was struggling to make advancements in my career. I thought I had reached my peak. Of course I could find another job that paid as much, or more, than the one I currently held. Subconsciously, I had run headlong into the fixed-mindset trap.

What is so interesting is I had no idea how I had gotten to this point. I used to live paycheck to paycheck as an actress. I would pick up double shifts to make payments so the government wouldn't repo my car. Hell, when I was living in Miami in 2003, if I didn't have money for food, I'd pretend I was interested in how Houston's, the restaurant where I waited tables, made the food and attend taste plate, an event where the chef fixes all the items on the menu and the general manager tastes each dish to approve or make recommendations before the restaurant opens. Sometimes I'd have half a baked potato and a five-nut brownie for breakfast, but I didn't care because later that day I'd be auditioning for a commercial or an indie film. Talk about commitment! I had a can-do attitude and always found a way to reach my goals.

Once upon a time, my dreams were so important that I prioritized them over money. Once upon a time, I'd had a growth mindset. What had changed? Where did it go? By 2017, I had suppressed it so deeply that I couldn't find it.

You may be able to recall a time when you had a growth mindset, but are you stuck in a fixed mindset now? Which areas of your life feel harder to change than others? It can be difficult to identify our fixed mindset when we're living in the midst of it. When I'm working with my clients, I can often uncover their fixed mindset based on the phrases they use and the thoughts they share with me during our coaching sessions. That's part of why having a coach or therapist is so valuable for women—so they can have a third-party view of the situation. While I can't sit down with you for a session while you're reading this, how about a quick private quiz to help gauge where you are today?

Please note that this quiz is not a definitive measure of mindset and is intended only as a guide.

1. **When faced with a difficult challenge, do you tend to:**
   - A Give up easily and assume you're not good at the skill the challenge requires?
   - B Keep trying and believe that you can improve with effort?

2. **When you receive feedback or criticism, do you tend to:**
   - A Feel defensive and take it personally?
   - B View it as an opportunity for growth and learning?

3. **When you encounter someone who is better than you at something, do you tend to:**

    A Feel jealous or intimidated?

    B Feel inspired to learn from them so you can improve yourself?

4. **When you encounter a setback, do you tend to:**

    A View it as a reflection of your abilities and give up?

    B See it as a learning opportunity and try again, taking a new approach?

5. **When you encounter a new and unfamiliar task, do you tend to:**

    A Avoid it and stick with what you know?

    B Embrace it as a chance to learn something new and expand your skill set?

6. **When you achieve a success, do you tend to:**

    A Believe that it was purely luck or a one-time event?

    B Recognize your effort and hard work that led to your success?

Scoring: Count up the number of A and B responses you gave. If you have mostly As, you may have a fixed mindset. If you have mostly Bs, you may have a growth mindset. Don't stress too hard if you discovered you have a fixed mindset. Armed with this information, you can take back control of your circumstances. You already know a growth mindset can be developed over time with practice and effort. Keep going, girlfriend; put in the work!

All is not lost if you've fallen into a season of fixed mindset. I find that our mindset can ebb and flow with the circumstances and seasons of our lives. Not that we ever want to intentionally abandon a growth mindset, but it can clearly happen, as you've seen from my real-life example.

When I found myself in a fixed mindset, I did the work, taking the steps to change how I looked at my life. (Newsflash: that's one of the few things in this world you can actually fully control!)

Shifting from a Fixed to a Growth Mindset: How to Begin

When I began the work to shift from a fixed to a growth mindset, first, I made a commitment to myself. A commitment to change. (Does this sound familiar from Chapter 3?) I wrote it down and read it over and over:

> *If I am still at this company in a year, I will have failed myself. I know I am capable of more.*

The idea of failing myself was too great not to follow through on and was an intrinsic motivator. As a general rule I don't suggest using negative words in your affirmations or change statements. You don't want your brain to associate your goal with a negative word—in this case, failure. With that said, remember, this was before I had been formally trained as a coach. Fortunately, my negatively worded change statement still worked! I then used SMART Goal construction to give myself a realistic timeframe to make a game plan and get out of my uninspiring job. Just that little shift in mindset helped me be open to the signs the Universe was sending me and have a more optimistic view.

You can start shifting your own mindset by becoming hyperaware of your fixed-mindset beliefs. I often invite my clients to carry around a notebook for a week and jot down every fixed-mindset belief they can identify. What traps are you falling into? Take note. Have you caught yourself thinking:

> *I'm not cut out for this job because I don't have enough experience.*

> *I can't balance work and family, so I'll never be able to achieve my goals.*

> *I'm not good at prioritizing my time and managing my workload.*

> *I don't have the skills or abilities to advance in my career.*

> *I can't ask for help because that would make me look weak.*

By recognizing these thoughts and reframing them into growth-mindset thoughts, you can develop a more positive and productive mindset. For instance, instead of thinking, *I don't have the skills or abilities to advance in my career*, you might think, *I have a hunger to learn and improve, and I will attain those skills in time.*

You're also welcome to adopt the "If/then" structure I shared earlier, but it's not a requirement. Some examples could be, *If I hit my revenue goal in the first year of my business, then I'll be able to leave my nine-to-five job*; or *If I hit my goal weight by Christmas, then I'll treat myself to a vacation.*

When I got a call from a recruiter two months after I set my change statement, I jumped at the chance to interview. The interview was for a role in a totally different industry, so it was my first tendency to doubt myself, to let my inner critic run wild with all the reasons why I wouldn't be a good fit. However, focusing on my new way of thinking, I replaced those thoughts with more helpful beliefs: *Of course they will want to hire me. I can bring a fresh perspective and best practices from the tech industry to the energy industry. I have a lot of knowledge to share and proven processes to build out this new division's marketing team.*

The next active thing I did that my fixed mindset would have seen as ill-advised was that I asked for help as I prepped for my interview. I know asking for help can feel scary and vulnerable, and yet that's exactly what a growth mindset demands of us—getting out of our comfort zone. Our society tells us people who succeed in America have pulled themselves up by their own bootstraps.... That's not only illogical but also physically impossible! You're probably familiar with the old quote, "Behind every man is a strong woman," but behind some of our most successful politicians, executives, and celebrities is a whole team of people—coaches, trainers, media reps, friends and family for emotional (and financial) support, and so on. Not asking for help and thinking strength and independence mean strict self-reliance is actually, in its own way, a fixed mindset that's holding so many bright, talented women back.

In my case, I leveraged my dad, who spent his whole career in utilities. I also messaged former colleagues who had transitioned to the energy sector and asked them for introductions to insightful, influential people in the field. I was not shy or embarrassed about asking these questions, something my fixed mindset surely would have prevented me from doing in the past.

After acing the interviews, I was offered the role. Most people would have been ecstatic and taken the offer at face value. In true growth-mindset fashion, though, I wanted to negotiate. I wanted to be certain I was getting the *best* offer. This is not some crazy success story where they added another $20,000 to my salary. Instead, the hiring team confirmed they were at the top of the pay scale already and couldn't budge. Nevertheless, I was earning about $15,000 more a year than I was in my previous role, had a higher bonus and unlimited PTO, all while managing a smaller team. I was satisfied that I really did get the best package they could offer me.

Before doing anything else, I celebrated my win. This is critical to the shift from fixed to growth mindset, as it serves as positive reinforcement that your new way of living is rewarding. I took my family out to a fancy dinner and raised a toast to my new role. You might do something else when you reach a milestone in your growth-mindset journey, such as end work an hour early, treat yourself to a special lunch, or go on a weekend getaway. What seemed like an impossible feat—getting a new job that would reenergize me, pay me what I was worth, and give me an opportunity to grow my skill set—was now my reality. And all I had to do was tap into my growth mindset to get there.

While my new job was a great win in the moment, it was only the first step on the path to my current level of fulfilment—and to where I ultimately envision myself. This first step to unlocking my growth mindset encouraged me to take other calculated risks and actions as I later explored life coaching as a new career path, moved my family to a different state, and began to write books. (Remember the domino effect?) To do that, I performed another version of asking for help—surrounding myself with like-minded people, especially others who were at my level or further ahead on the path to my goal.

This is another helpful approach to show you that what you desire is possible! Pro tip: your network matters. Want to get in shape? Hang out with people who are active and in shape. Want to make it to the C-suite? Fill your network with those in C-level roles. Want to deepen your spirituality? Socialize with people steeped in faith. Motivational speaker Jim Rohn famously said that we are the average of the five people we spend the most time with. Who are you spending your time with? Are they helping you develop a growth mindset? If so, bravo. If not, and you feel that their fixed mindset or gloomy demeanor is dragging you down, it may be time to make some changes. Not everyone is worthy of your time. Not everyone will make the cut.

When That Fixed Mindset Just Won't Jimmy Loose

I know some of you might be thinking, "Seriously, Karin? 'Just switch it up! Be positive! That growth mindset will come!' Yeah, right. It's not that easy." I hear you…but I'm also here to tell you that line of thinking is a classic limiting belief. With that said, because I'm rooting for you and because I understand that a positive mindset can be easier for some to achieve than others, let me offer some practical guidance to help you free yourself from that fixed mindset you're stuck in.

Let's look at a concrete example that you might be facing. What if you want to leave your job to start a business but you're worried about your finances? In your head that probably sounds pretty scary. (It did for me at first too.) A little planning goes a long way, so you might move from feelings to facts. Take a look at your finances to see where you can trim the fat. What expenses could you do without? What subscriptions could you cancel? You could probably get by with a lower salary and better hours, for instance, if you stopped going out to eat every Friday night.

We'll talk more about risk mitigation in the next chapter, "Create Unshakable Confidence," but you can also ask yourself, "What is the worst-case scenario here?" You might be worried you'll blow through your life savings getting your company off the ground, but by shifting your mindset, you can explore a different question: "How can I avoid losing all my savings?" That probably looks like saving up a nest egg before you launch, putting a limit on how much of your own money you'll invest, getting a partner, or even buying a business that already turns a profit.

Now that you see how you can effectively overcome your fear by addressing it head-on, you should be better able to say, "What could be possible? How could I make this happen?"

Once you've started to pry yourself lose from that fixed mindset, here are some solid steps to follow to put your growth mindset into action.

Commit to change. What changes do you need to move away from a fixed mindset right now? Write them down. Stare at your answers. Say them out loud. If you're not sure, ask someone you trust for honest feedback. If they are a good friend or care about you, they will be honest. Just be ready to hear and receive the feedback rather than to take it as a personal affront.

Change your vocabulary. What words or phrases are you using that are limiting you? Are you saying, *I couldn't possibly, I'd never be able to, I'm not smart enough,* or *I'm too old?* Consider rethinking those. You might change them to something like, *I probably could, I might be able to, I'm pretty smart,* or *Age doesn't matter.* Avoid words like "should" and "have to," and instead employ words like "want to" and "get to." Similarly, avoid constructions that include negative words like "not." Our brains don't grasp smaller words like that, so they'll get stuck on what you're not going to do anymore. For instance, instead of saying, "I'm not going to live in fear anymore," try switching to the bolder, more exciting, "I'm going to move forward, brave and confident in my abilities." I have a powerful exercise in the "Make It Happen" section that will help you with changing your negative self-talk so your vocabulary matches your healthy mindset.

Change your perspective. At this point, after you've made a change statement, most people will start with the what-ifs…. *What if I fail? What if people think I'm crazy? What if I don't make enough money?* But, hey, do you notice something? That's right! Those are always negative scenarios. Instead, turn those what-ifs around and make them positive. *What if I succeed? What if people think I'm a genius? What if I make more money than I earn now?* See the difference there? A positive outlook naturally leads to a growth mindset. If these positives seem too much like flights of fancy at the early stages of your shift to a growth mindset, remember to ask yourself, "Okay, worst-case scenario, what's going to happen if I take this chance?" Often when we voice our fears, we realize they aren't as big and scary as they seemed in our heads.

Ask for help. How many of us are afraid to ask for help? How many of us feel embarrassed or like we are a burden? I've been there. Let me ask you this: How does it feel to help a friend, colleague, or family member? When I ask clients, they always gush about how great helping someone out makes them feel. With this in mind, how do you think the people you ask for help feel? Chances are they feel fulfilled, with a sense of joy that they've proven useful in some way. Stop robbing others of this joy. Let them help you. By doing so, you'll be helping yourself too.

Celebrate the win. Celebrating is a super important step when you're making a change. Unfortunately, it's a step that most women ignore. We're always pushing ourselves from one thing to the next, glossing over our accomplishments as if they were nothing. You wouldn't hike to the top of a mountain and immediately turn to the next one without enjoying the scenery, would you? No! Stop, take a breather, and enjoy this moment. You've earned it.

Surround yourself with others who are doing what you want to do. One of the best things I did when I became a coach was surround myself with other coaches. I quickly saw I was not alone in some of my struggles, and as a result, I realized that what I was experiencing was normal. I was also able to learn faster from coaches who were further along than me. Be mindful if you start to play the comparison game and fall into fixed thinking again. As long as you look at your colleagues' achievements from a sense of comradery and support, it will be very helpful for you to see others succeeding in your area of interest.

We've covered a lot of ground in this chapter, and as you know, changes like this don't happen with a snap of our fingers. Your brain might even be swirling as you ponder all that your mindset makeover entails.

I would encourage you to take a deep breath and address it one step at a time. You don't have to master this overnight;

you probably couldn't even if you tried. Just becoming aware of your fixed mindset and committing to revamp it into a growth mindset is a huge win worth celebrating. As you tackle each fixed thought, you'll be strengthening your growth mindset. With a growth mindset in action, you'll be well on your way to grabbing life by the dreams, and you can build your own confidence, as we'll cover in the next chapter.

For now, check out the "Make It Happen" section below for one of my favorite exercises to encourage a mindset shift.

• •

Make It Happen

Releasing the Lies

I love this exercise because I've seen the power it's had in my life and the lives of my clients. Grab a piece of paper or your journal and let's get to work!

1. *Start by identifying a fixed-mindset thought.* For example, "I'm not good at math," "I'll never be able to learn a new language," or "I'm not creative."

2. *Once you've identified the fixed-mindset thought, reframe it into a growth-mindset thought.* For example, "I may not be good at math yet, but I can learn with practice and effort," "Learning a new language may be challenging, but I'm capable of learning and improving," or "I can develop my creativity with practice and experimentation."

3. *Practice the new belief.* Now that you've reframed the thought, practice it by repeating it to yourself and incorporating it into your daily life. I often recommend my clients practice in front of a mirror so they can look at themselves while they say the words. For example, when you're faced with a math problem, remind yourself that you can learn with practice and effort. Over time, the new belief will become more automatic and natural.

4. *Regularly reflect on your progress and celebrate small victories.* Recognize areas where you've demonstrated a growth mindset and identify areas where you can continue to work on adopting a growth mindset.

Chapter 8

Create Unshakable Confidence

*You gain strength, courage, and confidence by every
experience in which you really stop to look fear in the
face. You are able to say to yourself, "I have lived through
this horror. I can take the next thing that comes along."
You must do the thing you think you cannot do.*

—ELEANOR ROOSEVELT, *YOU LEARN BY LIVING:
ELEVEN KEYS FOR A MORE FULFILLING LIFE*

It was my first time being invited on the company jet. We
were headed to a charity event in Pittsburgh for the morning,
and we'd be back by midafternoon. On the one hand, it was
a dream come true. I'd finally made it high enough in the

company to warrant accompanying an executive in style. On the other hand, I was terrified the little plane would crash and my last moments would be spent with people who really didn't give a crap about me. Since it was a quick, routine flight, I pushed the morbid thought out of my brain and relished my moment to shine.

As I walked up to the plane, I was joined by a man from the PR team who would be escorting me and the division president for the day. Once onboard, I stood in the aisle, dumbfounded as to what to do next. Intuitively I knew there had to be a designated seat for the president.

"Where does he normally sit?" I questioned.

"I don't know. Just sit anywhere." He waved his hand to the right side of the plane.

Because I get motion sickness, I took the first front-facing chair. The last thing I wanted was to be puking my guts out in front of the president.

I kept myself busy checking emails until he arrived. Five minutes before we were set for "wheels up," he came waltzing through the jet door. Without a moment's hesitation, he slid his glasses down the bridge of his nose and said, "You're in my seat."

My cheeks now the color of a ripe tomato, I fumbled to grab my things. I took the opportunity to shoot the PR guy a death stare for not warning me I had chosen the president's seat, but before I could mutter, "I'm sorry," the president waved me off, saying, "No, no. Don't move. I'll sit here."

Phew! Well, at least I thought it was a "phew" moment. He then proceeded to lecture me on plane etiquette for the next five minutes. Turns out since I was the most junior person on the plane I should have been all the way at the back by the bathroom. I sat still, a smile plastered on my face so as not to show my embarrassment, nodding along to his monologue.

Stupid me! Why would I have sat at the front of the plane. It's not junior high. The cool kids don't sit at the back of the bus. I guess it's obvious that I don't belong here after all. I'm never taking the jet again.

If I didn't have feelings of self-doubt and imposter syndrome before I got on that plane, I sure as shit did now! What should have been a little blip on my career radar had now turned into a full-scale attack on my confidence.

What Confidence Isn't

Unfortunately, I'm not the only woman who has had her confidence shaken in the corporate world. Whether it's sexual harassment, being talked over in meetings, or being called "kiddo" well into your thirties, the confidence crushers come in a variety of forms. Bit by bit, negative comment after negative comment, and embarrassing situation after embarrassing situation, our self-assurance is eroded away until there's barely anything left. It's pretty hard to grab life by the dreams without confidence, huh?

A lot has been said about confidence over the years. What is it? How does one acquire it? Can you lose it? If so, can you get it back? Perhaps you were looking for a bit of Disney Princess magic here. A wave of a wand, some sparkle dust, and a fairy godmother to chant bibbidi-bobbidi-boo. What I'm going to propose will actually be easier to implement and far faster to come by.

Many women think confidence is something you're born with, but, if we learned anything in the last chapter, we know that with our growth mindset we can learn *anything*, including confidence. It's also a common misconception that you must be missing a key ingredient if embracing confidence doesn't come naturally to you. Wrong! If that were true, then we'd be back to the notion of being born with it and that everything should come easily. What examples from your life can you think of where a skill was hard at first, but you learned to master it over time?

Others will say confidence is a feeling. Have you ever said something like, "When I have more experience, then I'll *feel* confident"? This is not so. Feelings are fleeting. Confidence is something that should be a mainstay, strong and steady, not a passing feeling to be sought after. I'm sure you can once again think of a time you accomplished something and expected your confidence to soar but, at the first sign of trouble or conflict, immediately got down on yourself again.

Confidence is further misconstrued as arrogance or cockiness, especially when it's coming from strong, assertive women who may feel like they have to tone down their self-assurance to seem easier, safer. Have you ever received feedback during a performance review that you're too direct or even come across as aggressive? When that happens, women may choose to alter their approach and subdue their confidence, whether consciously or subconsciously. After all, no one wants to come off as cocky or overbearing! Usually this isn't actually the case, but we can be shamed into feeling like it is.

Some people say confidence is a personality trait. They attribute confidence to extroverts, thereby assuming that, since they are introverted, they can't possibly possess the same amount of confidence that others do. While it's true that extroverts are social creatures who get energy from being around others, there is no science to back up the claim that extroverts are more confident. Read that again: there is no scientific proof that extroverts are more confident than introverts. Plenty of extroverts lack confidence, and introverts can be extremely confident even though they prefer to spend their free time in smaller groups or alone with their thoughts.

Take a moment to journal on the following questions: Would you classify yourself as an extrovert or introvert? What false beliefs have you been consciously or subconsciously associating with your personality style? What are some of your own misconceptions about confidence? How can you myth-bust them now?

Lack of confidence comes in a variety of unfortunate flavors. It can look like not taking credit for your hard work, attributing your success to luck, or constantly feeling like you're not smart enough and trying to acquire more knowledge to compensate. It can result in not speaking up for yourself or advocating for your needs, in putting others first (to a fault), and in ignoring your intuition. When we live in a state of low confidence, we're more likely to feel stuck, and that's never an enjoyable place to be.

For many women, a lack of confidence takes root at an early age. Here's what my client Celina had to say on this matter:

> *The way I was raised, the cultural influences in Latin America that I experienced as a young girl, and other, later-in-life experiences led me to misunderstand what confidence really means. I had a tendency to lower my head, to agree easily, to give in, and [I] justified it by accepting it all as humility, a trait I was raised to uphold, to work toward. I also felt that I did not want to satisfy my Ego, fearing the outcome. I've been mindful of the dangers that Ego invites into one's life. The combination of my focus on humility and the fear to overfeed my Ego were the reasons I did not work on my own confidence for a long time; they were the excuses and the lies I told myself. I knew it would be a complex undertaking as a survivor of thirteen years of domestic violence, and someone whose identity was shattered after her corporate career of fifteen years abruptly ended.*

Like Celina, you may be laboring under some, or maybe even all, of the misconceptions of what confidence is that we've covered above. If you are, then it is critical to your success that you break them down and replace them with a healthier alternative. I hope that the reframing definition offered in the next section can help.

A New Definition for Confidence

Are you ready to start with a fresh perspective? To throw out everything you thought you knew about confidence? (Yes, everything!) Good, because this is going to change your life.

By taking a new approach and subscribing to a new definition of confidence, we are better able to embody this highly important trait. Remember to put your growth-mindset glasses back on if you've taken them off—it's important that you look at the following definition through those eyes:

> *Confidence* **is a deep trust in your own capabilities and a desire to try something new or different, understanding that even if things don't work out as intended, you'll have learned something in the process.**

Before we go on, read that definition a few more times. What do you think about its message? What about it stands out as different from your previous conception of confidence? I hope this is blowing your mind. It blew mine when I first came to understand it.

This new definition takes away all the external factors and misconceptions we went over at the top of the chapter and instead places the ability to have and exude confidence in your hands (i.e., "your own capabilities"). In doing so, it takes away any pressure you might have felt based on the false idea that confidence goes hand in hand with perfection. What problem or challenge have you figured out successfully before? How did you navigate it? If you fell down and got back up again, that in itself was confidence in your ability to tackle the problem from another angle. Put another way, the journey to success is very rarely a straight line, and if you have prior experience with course-correcting, you can certainly do it over and over again.

By trusting in your own capabilities, you will also stop looking at others and wishing you possessed something they have. Chances are they look at you, too, wishing they had one of your many talents! The comparison game is a waste of precious time and energy and will only rob you of your confidence. This definition invites you to focus only on *your* amazing skill set.

The definition goes on to say that a confident person has "a desire to try something new or different." Do you have that desire? You must, or you wouldn't still be reading this book! We already know change is growth, so let's embrace the fact that throughout life we are going to need to change and do things differently than before. Think about one of the many changes you've been through already. Even in the face of a big change or challenge, you can see how you've come out on the other side for the better, having learned something in the process.

Now is a great time to go back to your journal and ponder a few more questions: What do you think about this definition of confidence? How would you define confidence for yourself? Reviewing your personal definition, how can you apply its tenets in everyday life?

The concept of cognitive behavioral therapy (CBT) can be helpful here. CBT suggests that your thoughts impact your feelings and your feelings drive your actions. This is known as the *cognitive triangle.*

Let's consider this with a practical example. Imagine you had a big presentation coming up at work. You might be thinking, *If I fail, I'm going to blow my chances at a promotion.* You begin to feel worry or self-doubt. As a result, you stay up all night practicing and running through your slide deck, and you lose sleep. The next morning you're exhausted, hit snooze too many times, and are late for your presentation, thereby manifesting the outcome you were trying to avoid.

Now let's imagine you were my coaching client. While I'm not a licensed therapist, I'd start by asking you how you could change your thoughts about confidence, particularly as it applies to your presentation. Perhaps you'd realize this isn't your only chance to progress in your career, that your track record is strong and you have results from recent projects that make you a likely candidate for promotion. You might begin to feel relief and even excitement about the presentation. Instead of seeing it as determining the fate of your entire career, you might reframe it as a chance to showcase your hard work. You might run through the presentation once at night before bed and once again in the morning, ensuring you get your needed rest and still put ample prep work in, resulting in you showing up to work on time, refreshed, and prepared for the day ahead.

Similarly, with the help of a new definition and CBT-based tools, your feelings about confidence can be changed simply by changing your thoughts. If you regularly think that you are more confident and reframe your lived experiences in this definition, then over time, you will come to feel it is true. Sounds a lot like the manifesting work we discussed earlier, doesn't it? What thoughts around your own confidence would you like to change? Why? Write down a few that come to mind, but leave space as you identify additional ones in the coming days and weeks.

Six Tips to Creating Unshakable Confidence

What does having confidence allow you to do? You mean besides becoming the badass superwoman you were meant to be? Anything and everything!

Without negative thoughts to hold you back and keep you stuck, you're free to take steps toward your biggest dreams. So let me pass on my empowerment torch and give you six tips to help you build that unshakable confidence. Why unshakable? Well, because if it's not unshakable, then it's not really confidence.

1. *Shed your self-doubt.*

In order to move forward, you need to start by overcoming your self-doubt. These feelings of inadequacy are holding you back. Sure, it's normal to have some reservations when making a big change or taking on a new challenge, but when it becomes debilitating, it needs to be addressed. Seek to identify the source of your self-doubt. What do you believe is its root cause? Where is it coming from? Is it based on past experiences or negative self-talk? Understanding the source can help you develop strategies to overcome it.

Here's a helpful visualization exercise to help you overcome your self-doubts.

- Find a quiet place, free of any distractions, where you can relax in comfort.
- Close your eyes and take a few deep breaths, inhaling through your nose and exhaling through your mouth.
- Picture yourself standing alone in front of a full-length mirror. Look at yourself and observe the thoughts and emotions that come up.
- Now, imagine that you are peeling off a layer of self-doubt from your body. Which specific doubt(s) are held within that layer? Start with your head and work your way down, peeling off each layer until you reach the bottom of your feet.
- As you peel off each layer, imagine that you are shedding their related negative thoughts and

limiting beliefs about yourself. See them falling away from you.

∾ Once you've peeled off all the layers, take a step back and look at yourself again in the mirror. Notice how you feel and what you see.

∾ Visualize yourself as a confident, capable, and empowered woman. See yourself achieving your goals and dreams. Take a moment to feel proud of yourself, knowing deep down this is the real you.

∾ Stay in this visualization for as long as you like, soaking up the feelings of confidence and self-belief.

When you're ready, take a few deep breaths and slowly open your eyes. How do you feel? Journal about the layers that you shed and how you felt at the end of the visualization. You can come back to this journal entry as often as needed to remind yourself of what you've let go of and who you are now. If you feel that you've gone through a period of personal growth, you might even repeat the visualization and journaling exercises to meet who you are today.

2. *Own your current situation.*

Go ahead and love your whole self, even the messy bits! Maybe you were laid off from your last job. Maybe you're newly divorced and starting over. Maybe you bombed your last interview or had a falling-out with your friend.

You're human. We all are. Don't let your mistakes define you. Instead, go ahead and own who you are in the frame of your current capabilities. Own your circumstances and your choices. No more apologizing. No more worrying about the skills and experience you don't have (yet).

How do you do this? Start by looking at your top accomplishments and the strengths you *do* possess. We all have our own strengths, so don't spend even one moment thinking you don't. If you find room for improvement, acknowledge it, but otherwise don't give it your energy right now. No one expects you to have all the answers all the time. (Perfectionists, pay attention here.) Not even the CEO of a Fortune 500 company has all the answers—that would be humanly impossible—but she doesn't have to. That's why she hires a stellar team who can fill in her weaknesses, allowing her to capitalize on her best skills. Maybe all you need is a keen ability to identify key skills in someone else to complement your own.

Imagine you're in a new role, leading a large team. You're looking to expand your product into a new geography you're unfamiliar with. No problem. You'd simply scan the team and see who has the experience you're missing. They could reverse-mentor you, or you could assign them as project lead. If no one on the team has that knowledge, put together a business case to hire someone that does. The sign of a confident, savvy leader is the ability to surround oneself with talented people and not feel threatened. The same goes for any profession, whether you're an aspiring entrepreneur, an author, or a doctor. Get curious, ask questions, and place yourself in the company of others doing what you hope to achieve.

When you own your current capabilities, rather than being embarrassed or shamed by them, you'll find you're a lot more confident when it comes to moving out of your comfort zone. And look! Now you can add resourceful to your list of capabilities.

3. Face your fear(s).

We all have fears. Fear is healthy and normal. The key, though, is to work through your fear instead of letting it hold you back. Fear only has power if we let it have power, and when we acknowledge our fears and choose to name them, we instantly make them less powerful.

What fears have been swirling around your head? They're often a lot scarier when we leave them in our brain for our inner critic to dissect and play on repeat. You're better off writing your fear(s) down and evaluating them. Once you have your fear on paper, ask yourself: How bad could it really be? Is this fear even valid? How might I mitigate this fear?

Let's say you want to get back into the gym regularly. You might be scared about going because you don't know how to use all the machines or you're worried people will judge how you look. While these fears can feel powerful in your head, once you write them down, they lose their power. Are you willing to let your health and well-being suffer because you're worried about being judged? Hell no! You're going to laugh in the face of fear, strut into the gym, and figure it out.

Another helpful tactic for addressing your fears can be to remind yourself why you're making a change in the first place. You were given *a desire* for a reason. Recall our definition of confidence. In it, the word "desire" refers to you wanting to actually face this new idea, project, or challenge you're presented with. There's a willingness in you to go the extra mile and give it a try. If you're forced into the family business, no matter how much you trust your own capabilities, if there's no desire, it's unlikely you'll come across as confident, much less be confident in yourself. Alternatively, if you can't wait to launch a new makeup line you've developed, there will be an automatic, fear-defying, confidence-boosting desire that no one can extinguish. It will drive you to try at all costs, against all odds.

Sharon Lechter, author and keynote speaker, describes this in *Think and Grow Rich for Women* as "your burning desire": "It may feel like a need to do something or accomplish something. It starts out as an idea or realization and grows to become a driving force behind your everyday actions." Having a burning desire gives you the ability to fight your fears.

In discussing our sessions together, my coaching client Erin shared her experience with fears:

> *The fear of failure and fear of judgment has been so enormous, but Karin has been right next to me as I take giant leaps to stay focused on myself and not let those fears derail me. My biggest advice is to always show up no matter what; do not let fear stand in your way. The right opportunity is out there for you. Just stay consistent, be authentic, believe in yourself, and ask for help.*

Avoiding fear or lying to ourselves won't make the situation any better. Be honest with yourself about what truly scares you, address it, and then if it still feels scary, commit to facing it anyway. Step four will help here as well.

4. Make a plan.

Most women never get to this step because they let fear get in the way. Once you know your fears, it's time to make a game plan to address them. Begin by identifying the areas that you need the most support in and find resources that can help you. This might require you to take a class or find a mentor. It's unlikely you're the first to ever face this challenge, so there should be plenty of resources available.

You can make a plan not only for how to address your fears, but also for how to mitigate risk. One of my clients, Mary Beth, recently wanted to leave behind a toxic professional environment for a better corporate culture. When she received a job offer, though, she had fears that the new company, which was in the same industry, would have just as poor of a culture. She worried she'd take the job and hate it. Through our coaching sessions, she was able to make a plan to mitigate that risk, which included meeting with current employees of the company in several departments, as well as speaking with the hiring leader during the interview process about this specifically.

The result? Her fears evaporated when she heard how positively everyone spoke about the company. She confidently accepted the role and loves her new challenge as senior director of commercial marketing. She now firmly gives the following advice to other women: "Don't let fear of the unknown hold you back." Having a plan, like Mary Beth's plan to gather more information and clearly express her professional needs, makes it a whole lot easier to overcome your fears and move forward.

5. Fake it till ya make it.

It's the one area of life where I say it's okay to fake it! In the bedroom? No. In the boardroom? Hell yes!

It's important that we're clear on what we're faking, though. We're not suppressing our feelings or emotions or tolerating a toxic situation. If you're unhappy, that's a clear signal that something needs to change. What I'm suggesting is that, when you're lacking confidence in a particular area, you pretend as though you already have the confidence you desire.

I remember attending an event for female professionals in telecom at which a senior leader was asked how she handled being the first woman on her executive team. She divulged that she had had her share of nerves, but she faked her confidence until it became real. She couldn't have known what a relief it was to hear her confess that. In that one sentence, my feelings, and those of many other audience members, were normalized. If she was still faking it at the C-level, then surely I could fake it at mine. And you can too!

Did you ever want to be an actress when you were younger? If so, consider this your big break! If a client is feeling performance-related nerves, I encourage them to imagine they're playing a character in a movie. How would you handle the situation if you were that character? What would they say or do? Then try it on for size.

Another question you can ask yourself is, What would the most successful and confident version of me do in this situation? That's a powerful question. Use the answer to act as if you know what you're doing. I think you'll surprise yourself with how quickly you can trust that you're making the right moves and the right decisions. It can feel a little strange at first, but with some practice, this can become second nature. Before long, you won't be acting—you will have grown into the role.

6. Use positive self-talk.

Unfortunately, there will always be someone who will want to undermine you, create doubts, and sabotage your success. Just make sure it isn't you!

Don't allow negative thoughts about yourself to creep into your mind or, worse yet, leave your mouth and sow seeds of doubt about you in others. You get to take on the role of being your biggest cheerleader. Put that inner voice to work in a positive way by transforming your self-talk. You're a fabulous, talented, powerful woman! Be your biggest champion and watch as others join in the chorus of praise.

Remember my client Celina? You might be wondering how she turned her confidence around. Here's what she has to say about how our time working together created real change for her:

> *Karin's Three-Day Challenge Creating Unshakable Confidence helped me to clearly see the successes I have experienced. She taught me to appreciate my wins, to look back and celebrate them, and to remind myself of them when necessary. The course helped me identify the negative self-talk that kept me stuck, feeling unworthy, like I was nothing special. Turning the lies I told myself into my new truths that make me a unique, kickass woman was like emerging from a cocoon, with butterfly wings spread wide open, sparkling in mesmerizing colors.*

There is no silver bullet to give you the confidence you deserve. The key to confidence is creating a habit of having it. It's about taking steps, no matter how small, and realizing you are strong enough to keep going. Each little win will validate you and strengthen your confidence for the next decision or challenge you face.

So, with a deeper understanding of this new definition and the steps to create a habit of confidence, you're ready to apply it to your life. You go, girlfriend!

• •

Make It Happen

If you're ready to make confidence a daily habit, these exercises will bring about the right mindset and establish irrefutable proof that you deserve to be confident as you go after your dreams. This is a transformative exercise that can give you an injection of confidence when you need it most.

Affirmations for Confidence: As we learned above, our thoughts impact our feelings and our actions. Let's work on your thoughts by starting with positive affirmations. Self-talk won't change if you don't put in the work regularly to change it.

> Start by standing in front of a mirror. Read each line out loud to your reflection:
>
> ∞ I am worthy of success.
>
> ∞ I am blessed.
>
> ∞ I am talented.
>
> ∞ I am financially abundant.
>
> ∞ I am smart.
>
> ∞ I have a unique purpose.

Do this consistently for thirty days; do it every night before bed and again when you wake in the morning. Just watch how you start to change your subconscious and become not only softer on yourself but more confident in your capacity for change. You're welcome to adapt any of these affirmations to better suit your situation.

Change Diary: If you skipped this activity in Chapter 3, I'd highly encourage you to go back and complete it now. If you did take the time to complete it, why not go back and revisit your answers? Add new experiences that have happened since you first completed the exercise.

Positive Proof: Nothing helps bolster confidence like words of affirmation, so seek out positive proof of your performance, character, and appreciation. This will bolster your confidence, especially as it relates to your existing capabilities. You can do this by:

- Reading recommendations from your connections on LinkedIn.
- Reading your reviews of your book or for your business.
- Reading old notecards from appreciative clients or bosses.

Creating Confidence 3-Day Challenge:
If you'd like more support on confidence, you can sign up to take my 3-Day Challenge, which is available on demand: www.karinfreeland.com/confidence

Chapter 9

Find a Bigger Purpose

When you are bigger than your purpose you have a career.
When your purpose is bigger than you, you have a calling.

—JOHN C. MAXWELL

When Erin first came to me, she was stressed, confused, and overwhelmed. At the same time, she had big dreams, especially when it came to supporting women and leaving a legacy. She described her situation as follows:

> *"I was at a place where I really was just going through the motions of the day. After an incredibly successful career at a Fortune 500 company, I was on the job market again,*

> *experiencing rejection after rejection. I couldn't under-*
> *stand what I was doing wrong. Even though good things*
> *were happening with my book [a number one interna-*
> *tional bestseller], I couldn't get out of the cycle of feeling*
> *stuck, not being able to move forward or fully enjoy the*
> *present moment."*

Everything was swirling around in her head, but she wasn't sure how to put any of it into action. One of the first exercises I had Erin do was to write out all of her dreams and goals so we could get them out of her head and onto paper. Nothing was too big or too small to go on the list. When we regrouped to review her list, I quickly realized how strong her passion was for helping others. Although she had published her story to help others overcome grief, she wanted to have an even bigger impact on the world. As she listed a handful of charitable organizations she wanted to join to further her mission, I identified that volunteering would be an area where Erin could experience a quick win, especially after so much recent rejection, so we decided to tackle this goal first. However, she was exhibiting classic stuck behavior; overburdened by choice, she had chosen more organizations than she could possibly support at this time and therefore had been doing nothing. As homework, I had her research the organizations she felt most called to work with and shortlist the ones she was most compelled to support.

By our next session, she had whittled the list down to just two organizations, which she decided to sign up for. By our following session she had applied to both and was in the process of getting more deeply involved with them. What had seemed like an impossible feat (i.e., advancing her big goal of supporting women) was overcome with a little guidance, clear action steps, and intentional focus. Plus, she incurred the added benefit of a quick win, which motivated her to keep going and checking goals off her list. All of this was necessary to feed one very important human need: a bigger purpose for her life.

Finding Your Bigger Purpose

Do you have a calling? Chances are, if you don't feel like you have a bigger purpose, you're experiencing a sting—a sense that something's missing.

We all derive our sense of purpose in different ways and from different outlets. For some of us, it's the seemingly little things, like being the positive person at work or donating monthly to charity. Others may do seemingly big things, like stand on a stage and impact thousands of lives or invent a new, life-saving technology. Society will tell us that some purposes are bigger or better than others, but I disagree. If we're living in alignment with our purpose and having a meaningful impact on those around us, then our purpose is just as good as anyone else's. That's far better than squandering our potential impact out of fear and self-sabotage. (Besides, who are we to tell the Universe whose purpose is more valuable than another's?)

In many cases, not just Erin's, I've found that our sense of purpose is tied to a need to give back or leave the world better than we found it. In 2006, motivational speaker Tony

Robbins conducted research that led him to discover the six human needs, one of which is contribution. He determined that we will go to great lengths to fulfill these needs. If any of our needs go unmet, it can lead to those feelings of being stuck or lost in life. Even people who have reached what society would say is success may not be completely fulfilled if they are lacking in this department.

Purpose, or how you contribute, can be a tricky thing to latch onto. Many people think that if they are naturally good at something, that must be their purpose. But what happens when the thing you're good at isn't something you enjoy? Andre Agassi, arguably one of the world's best tennis players, wrote in his 2009 memoir, *Open*, "I play tennis for a living even though I hate tennis, hate it with a dark and secret passion and always have." Yikes! Who wants to be doing something, even for money, that you hate with a dark passion? Not me, and I bet not you!

One of the things I drive home with my clients is that talent doesn't always equal purpose. Just because you're a talented accountant doesn't mean you wouldn't be happier starting a nonprofit to help youth afflicted with juvenile rheumatoid arthritis. My client Brenda was a fabulous photo producer for several big-name firms, but she wasn't enjoying the rat race. Should she have stayed in her field, grinding away at something that no longer brought her joy, just because she was good at it? No way!

While your purpose can be manifested in any area of your life, like your career, it's far bigger than that. It's both internal and external, creating a warm feeling inside you while having a clear impact on the world around you. Some of you may have a keen sense of your purpose, your mission statement, in life. You might say, "I am here to make as many genuine human connections as I can," or, "I feel a strong connection to Mother Earth, and I want to do my part to keep her clean and unpolluted for future generations." And that's great.

But what if you *don't* know your purpose yet? Well, for one thing, that's totally understandable! In our day-to-day lives, it's hard to zoom out and consider big, existential mysteries, like what we were put on this earth to do. Purpose also ebbs and flows with the seasons of our life. Raising your children might have been your bigger purpose when they were toddlers, but now that they've gone off to college and you're an empty nester, you're likely seeking a new purpose.

If you want some help actively reflecting on your purpose, regardless of your season of life, try answering the following journal prompts:

- Think of a time where you felt most connected to the earth or to your fellow humans. Why did that moment fulfill you more than many others you have on a daily basis?
- Can you think of other moments like that one? What do these moments have in common that might reveal your bigger purpose to you?
- How can you use your unique strengths, talents, and passions to contribute to something meaningful?

What I love about these prompts is that different readers will answer them in any number of ways. You might have felt fulfilled when you've coordinated a big event from behind the scenes and therefore realize your purpose is firm, calm leadership under pressure. Or you might feel fulfilled by having a quiet heart-to-heart where your advice has a strong impact on a friend and therefore realize your purpose is giving others a safe space during the hard times. Even if they don't hand-deliver your purpose to you, your journal answers should turn on a few light bulbs that will help you eventually identify your bigger purpose and use it to create an impact in multiple areas of your life.

Using Your Bigger Purpose for the Greater Good

Now that you have a keener sense of your purpose, how can you fulfill it?

While it's true women can and do find purpose in their work by pursuing a career that aligns with their values and allows them to make a positive impact in their community or industry, a mistake a lot of us make is trying to realize our fulfillment and bigger purpose from our jobs *alone*. Well, as Mr. Agassi just vividly illustrated, if you're in a role you don't enjoy or secretly hate, how can you expect to feel fulfillment and purpose from it? I hate to burst your bubble, but it ain't gonna happen.

The bright side here is that your bigger purpose is—you guessed it!—bigger than any specific area of your life. For instance, if you find that your greater purpose is making as many genuine human connections as possible, you could apply this at work, by choosing a people-facing profession; in your family life, by taking a hands-on approach to parenting; or through volunteering, specifically in roles like helping out at a soup kitchen or shelter. If one area of your life isn't helping you feel very purposeful right now, perhaps it's time to try another on for size.

The examples that follow trend toward charitable means of using your purpose, such as volunteering and mentorship, and that's no coincidence. There are so many benefits, both personal and interpersonal, to volunteering, donating, and beyond.

For one thing, volunteering exposes you to different experiences, industries, and skill sets. You never know where this may lead you or how it will help you get unstuck. If you're feeling stuck without a sense of purpose in your career, then taking up a volunteer position will likely be the path of least resistance because the stakes are lower than changing your career altogether. Imagine volunteering at a local women's shelter and realizing you love working with underserved women and can use your corporate skills to lead fundraising for a nonprofit agency. Or imagine supporting a girls' camp focused on exposing young women to STEM careers and realizing you are uniquely positioned to join their board and expand their reach. Volunteering can take you down paths you never would have dreamed of taking! Those are baby steps that will naturally emerge if you're open to the options presented to you.

What's more, there are documented health benefits to volunteering. In one study conducted by Carnegie Mellon University and published in *Psychology and Aging*, researchers found that adults over fifty years old were less likely to develop high blood pressure when they volunteered on a regular basis. And it's not just our physical health that improves. According to the researchers, "[v]olunteering at least 200 hours was also associated with greater increases in psychological well-being." Your mental health will thank you too!

Finally, when you give back, you inspire others to do the same. By demonstrating the impact your purpose can have on the community, you encourage others to get involved and make a difference. Gotta love that ripple effect!

With all that in mind and without further ado, let's explore some charitable outlets in which you can apply your bigger purpose.

Volunteering

When I first moved to South Carolina, I didn't know a single soul. Since I worked from home, the opportunity to make new friends was minimal. I'm a social creature by nature, so this was a problem that needed to be remedied—*fast*. My real estate agent had mentioned a women's service organization called the Junior League. Being newly self-employed, my first thought was, *How much are dues?* I was pleasantly surprised when I heard the number and more pleasantly surprised when I realized—between my coaching and corporate background and our chapter's focus on economic mobility and stopping human trafficking—the impact I could have on our local community by joining the organization. My first year I spent over forty hours at our consignment store, The Nearly New Shop. I just loved placing the merchandise on the sales floor and seeing women in the community come in and select a purse or pair of shoes I'd put out that morning! It gave my life meaning beyond a paycheck and a title.

How could you give back and contribute to the world? Where could you volunteer? What talents could you share with others? There are so many organizations that need amazing people like you to help advance their mission, and the "Make It Happen" section at the end of this chapter contains tools to help you find the one(s) that is right for you.

It can be tempting to disqualify yourself from volunteering, using time as a scapegoat, but volunteering doesn't have to be something you do year-round. Many organizations have annual galas or fundraisers where they need extra hands on deck for a shorter window. In the end, we all have the same twenty-four hours in a day. Making an impact comes down to what you prioritize.

If your time really is too tight to add volunteering to your schedule, keep reading. I think you'll find the next outlet rather appealing for your time-crunched calendar.

Donating

Giving to others has a powerful effect on the soul. Some of us are blessed with disposable income, and while buying a new iPhone might be nice, think of the impact you could have on another person if you took some of that money and helped a life.

In my corporate days, time felt scarce. I now know that was merely a lack of prioritization and setting boundaries; nevertheless, it was easier and often just as helpful to give my resources instead of my time. As such, I participated in a number of food and supply drives in my town.

One morning, while hitting up the Dollar Tree for items on the latest list, my heart sank. I read aloud, under my breath, "Pads/Tampons." I did a double take. Did women really need pads and tampons? Of course they did. How could I have never thought about that before? If someone can't afford food for their family, how can they afford period products? I couldn't help but want to buy the entire shelf of period supplies. Years later, when I wrote my memoir, *The Ins and Outs of My Vagina*, I decided my book needed a bigger purpose too. I reached out to the Alliance for Period Supplies (APS) to inquire about donating a portion of the proceeds to their organization and including an ad for them in the back of the book. I've raised over $2,000 and counting for APS directly, but who knows what kind of impact I've had by sharing their message and raising awareness of period poverty? It's hard enough being a woman; we shouldn't have to worry about how we'll manage our period on top of it!

Another point of consideration is how much of your total income you want to donate annually. I remember looking at my expenses at the end of 2018 and being horrified by what I saw. I'd spent $4,368 on personal maintenance, and in the same timeframe I'd only tracked $83 in donations. That was, for lack of a better phrase, ass-backward! Fortunately, I was tracking my spending, so I could see the gaps and address them. In 2019, I got to a better (but not perfect) balance of $3,096 for looking glam and $1,280 for saving the world, and by 2022, I spent only $1,407 on my appearance and $902 in donations (not including what was donated to APS). God willing my business will grow and my giving will eventually surpass my personal maintenance threefold.

If you're gawking at those numbers, thinking, *There's no way I could find $1,200 to donate to charity this year*, that's totally fine. We all go through periods of boom and bust. If your cash reserves are a little low, why not consider all the *stuff* you have lying around that might be appropriate to donate? You could clean out a closet, call the Vietnam Veterans of America or another donation center the next time you get rid of a couch, or even donate proceeds from a yard sale to your favorite charity. Talk about benefits—by decluttering and donating your old items, you're multitasking on your to-do list!

Where do you feel called to donate and contribute? Take note and make a commitment to follow through today.

Mentoring

Have you benefited from having a mentor? What impact did they have on your life or career? Now think about what a big impact you could have on someone's life by becoming *their* mentor.

In my corporate career, I was honored to mentor several women over the years, some formally and some informally. Now, I focus on mentoring young people in my free time. My son's middle school announced a program called Adopt-a-Cougar. No, I'm not a mentor for a middle-aged woman who enjoys dating younger men! (Although that might be fun.) The school's mascot is a cougar, and they were seeking adults to mentor a group of at-risk seventh and eighth graders. Total no-brainer; it was in complete alignment with my values and made use of my life coaching skills. Once a month I bring my mentee lunch from her favorite restaurant and support her academically and personally. We talk about goal setting, proper eating and sleeping habits, even boyfriend drama.

There are lots of ways to get involved as a mentor. Check with your company to see if they have a formal mentor program you can join. Ask your local schools if they have a program similar to Adopt-a-Cougar, or consider starting one of your own.

Mentoring can also involve sharing your skills with someone else. I have a neighbor who is an excellent green thumb who has shown me how to improve my own garden. Maybe you're skilled at meditation or yoga and could teach a small group pro bono. By helping others fall in love with a sport or hobby, you can bring joy and meaning to their lives, just as that passion has brought joy to you.

No matter how you slice it, mentoring offers a powerful way to contribute to the world by uplifting and empowering others, fostering personal and professional growth, and creating a positive and lasting impact on individuals and communities.

Advocating for Social and Political Issues

Getting involved in advocacy work can be a powerful way to make a difference and feel a sense of purpose. This can involve supporting causes and policies that align with your values and beliefs. Look for a local march, phone-banking session, or 5K to participate in. Many organizations have diversity, equity, and inclusion committees or employee resource groups that you could consider participating in. Helping the workplace be a better environment for everyone is important work that will have a positive impact on generations to come.

Supporting Local Businesses

Supporting local businesses and entrepreneurs can help build and strengthen communities, create jobs, and support economic development. If you need a place to host a work meeting, choose a local restaurant instead of a chain. Need giveaways for a trade show? Order cookies with your logo from the local bakery.

Investing in Personal Growth

Our other examples have been community focused, but remember, you can't draw water from an empty well! This suggestion for how to find and use your purpose focuses entirely on Y-O-U.

Personal growth and development can provide us with a sense of purpose by helping us become the best versions of ourselves. Many women expect their company to foot the bill for their personal development, which usually means we get less of it than our male counterparts. Don't foist this responsibility on anyone else. You are responsible for your growth, whatever that looks like. Of course, hiring a coach can be a great step in the right direction and a worthwhile investment, especially since you'll be able to make the transformation faster.

Not to be morbid but, sadly, it only takes three to four generations for you to be forgotten after your death. (How's that for an "Oh, Shit!" Moment?) That's why having a purpose and leaving a legacy is so important to many women. A legacy is a way of ensuring that your impact on the world will continue long after you're gone. It's about creating something that will endure and be remembered for years to come.

For some, a legacy might mean leaving behind a successful business or foundation that will continue to thrive under new leadership. For others, it might mean contributing to a cause they're passionate about or making a significant impact on their community. Whatever form it takes, a legacy is a way of leaving your mark on the world and making a difference. It's one of the many reasons I wrote my first book. It was my way of solidifying that I was here on Earth.

Not all women will be driven to leave a legacy. Some may feel that the concept of leaving a legacy is too self-focused and that their impact on the world should be measured by the positive contributions they make to their communities and the people around them, rather than their long-term impact. Whatever you choose to do, be mindful of your motivation. Are you choosing something for status and notoriety, or is there an intrinsic drive? You may begin to resent volunteering, for example, if you're doing it for the wrong reasons.

As a high-achieving woman, there's no doubt you've had to break through significant barriers and overcome societal obstacles to achieve success. Once we've tended to basic needs like food, shelter, and success, many of us feel a sense of responsibility to give back and make a positive contribution to society. If that sentence resonated with you, consider this your time to find and then put to good use your bigger purpose.

• •

Make It Happen

If you want to volunteer but have never done so before, you might not know where to begin. A good starting point would be to research a few organizations that make your heart sing. Here are several questions to consider when choosing a cause to volunteer for or donate money to:

- Are they doing work that aligns with my values?

- What skills are they seeking that I could lend?

- What is their reach/service location?

- How do they use the funds that are received from donors?

- What kind of legacy do I want to leave? Does this align with that?

- How much money do I want to ideally be giving in charitable donations per year? What portion of that will go to this organization?

If you're not sure where you'd like to volunteer, check out Volunteer Match (www.volunteermatch.org), an online tool that connects nonprofits with individuals looking to donate their time. You'll quickly uncover the current needs in your local community.

Chapter 10

Own Your Power

*Being powerful is like being a lady. If you
have to tell people you are, you aren't.*

—MARGARET THATCHER

Did you know you are incredibly powerful?

Stop looking around and over your shoulder. Yes, I'm talking to *you*! Use whatever word you want—goddess, queen, badass—but you're all of that and a Louis Vuitton bag. You have so much inner strength and resilience that you haven't even begun to fully tap into. But when you do, the world better watch out—they've never seen anything like what you're about to bring! And I can't wait to watch it.

Some of you might be thinking, *Well, looks like Karin finally lost it. She had me up until that last paragraph.* And hey, if you are, I get it; it can be hard to hear complimentary things about ourselves and fully embrace our abilities.

But we're talking about more than confidence here. We're talking about expressing your personality without any apologies. No holds barred. Letting it all go and existing in your fullest being. There will be no more hiding the "ugly" parts or putting on a façade. Instead, there will only be total alignment between the inside and outside. This means standing up for yourself and pursuing your dreams and goals with determination and fortitude. It means owning your power!

Wait. What *Is* Owning Your Power?

I was first introduced to this concept of owning your power when I read Helene Lerner's book *In Her Power*. She defined *power* as "being able to act from a position of strength rather than react out of fear and limitation."

Can you think of a time in your life when you reacted (unnecessarily) out of fear? I have more than I care to count, but one stands out pretty vividly. When I was in the sixth grade, I was asked to audition for the local kids' news program. Being my dancing, outgoing self, I had no fear of performing, and yet I declined the offer. Why? Because I was terrified of what the other kids at school would think if they saw me on TV. I look back now and wish I could have talked some sense into twelve-year-old me. Who knows what might have come from that kind of experience and exposure?

Unfortunately, reacting from a place of fear isn't reserved for children. Every day women—very seasoned and accomplished women—are giving away their power, letting their inner critic drive the bus, and allowing fear to rob them of their full potential.

Why is it so hard for high-achieving women to own their power, or to change for that matter? I'll tell you why: It's precisely *because* we're so accomplished. We've done well in so many areas of our lives that we worry we'll make one wrong step and blow it all. We worry about failure, embarrassment, what others will think of us. Unfortunately, that's a lot of wasted energy. All that worrying accomplishes nothing—especially when it diminishes or limits your power.

Going from diminishing your power to owning your power doesn't happen overnight. It's a process that takes practice. And I'm not just talking the talk. I've been through this process a few times and have even made it a daily habit. (You can make it one, too, if you do the exercise in this chapter's "Make It Happen" section.) When I used to tell people my first book's title, I would brace myself, maybe wince a bit, waiting for their reaction. Sometimes I would even preface it with, "Don't let the title scare you…" or "Well, it's not for everyone, but…." Over time, though, I realized their reaction had nothing to do with me. That was on them. I found the courage to own my power and know that the right people would receive it with humor and open arms. I no longer needed to shrink behind my title. I could be the real me, no matter who I was around or what room I was in.

Are you ready to be the real you? Are you ready to unapologetically show up and own who you are 100 percent? Or does being the real you sound scary? It certainly might. Many high achievers I know are worried to be unashamedly, unapologetically, outspokenly themselves because they feel that others, who they think accept and respect them based on a false perception of themselves or only for their merits, no longer will. I've labored under this fear, too, but I'm here to tell you that what's on the other side of that fear is one of my favorite words: *freedom*. It's the freedom to be who you truly are, all day, every day. As the saying goes, "The people who matter won't mind, and the people who mind don't matter." You might have just let out a sigh of relief, like I did while I was writing this. Just the thought alone can bring a lowering of the shoulders and relaxing of tension you're holding in your body.

How to Own Your Power

If you're picking up what I'm putting down and want to start owning your power, here are some ways you could explore this.

Become Self-Aware

Most processes in coaching start with self-awareness, as they should. We can't improve what we don't understand, so by getting clear on where you're giving your power away, you'll have a better handle on what you need to address.

Usually this starts with little things, like saying you don't care what movie you watch for Friday date night and ending up with an action flick when you really had a romantic comedy on the brain or like not speaking up at work when you get removed from a meeting invite without warning. The problem with not being aware of these minor instances of relinquishing your power is they begin to morph into bigger and bigger concessions until we feel like we have no power at all. Hence, the overwhelming feeling of being stuck! By becoming aware of the situation and reclaiming your power one instance at a time, you can rebuild your strength in this area.

Speak Up for Yourself

Many women lack the assertiveness required to communicate their needs clearly. If this is you, I'd strongly advise that you get support in this area. It's bad enough that women get overlooked at work for not speaking up, but you don't want to have this happen in other areas of your life too!

Why does this being overlooked happen? Well, to put it plainly, you are not the center of anyone else's universe. I hope that last little bit of tough love didn't sting too badly, but if it did, you probably really needed to hear that. Although we think everyone should know exactly how we're feeling, they don't. You have to speak up and make your ambitions, desires, and wishes known.

A friend of mine got overlooked for a promotion. When she finally mustered up the courage to ask her boss why they didn't consider her for the role, he told her he had no idea she had been interested in it. Naturally she was furious, but the only person she had to be mad at was herself. She had been working herself to the bone under the delusion that someone would recognize her hard work and reward her accordingly. She'd never bothered to speak up and discuss her career goals with her boss, leaving him oblivious to her aspirations. What career ambitions do you need to voice?

And what about at home? If you're waiting for your husband to realize you want him to fold the laundry, you're going to be waiting a very long time. I agree it would be nice if our partners were mind readers and did things without being asked, but they don't work like that. Instead, we need to speak up. Ask him to do the laundry and let him know the outcome when he does it. Maybe you'll be in the mood for sex or have more time to help the kids with homework so he doesn't have to. If he still won't do it, take his laundry to the laundromat; I bet when he sees the bill, he'll start folding the laundry. Or he'll be so thrilled that neither of you had to do it, you'll be able to start budgeting for laundry service.

If speaking up for yourself sounds nerve-racking, start small. How many times does someone ask you, "Where do you want to go for dinner?" and you just shrug and say, "Wherever you want is fine." That's a minor example, but it illustrates the point of giving away your power. Instead, try giving options at first: "I'd prefer sushi or Mexican. Which one sounds better to you?" You know you're going to get either your first or second choice, and it might feel less demanding as you're getting your bearings. Eventually, you'll be able to confidently respond, "I want to try the new sushi joint downtown. I'll call ahead and get us a table." As you get more comfortable speaking up in a casual, day-to-day setting, you'll find it spills over into your career and other aspects of your life.

Set Healthy Boundaries

One of the biggest challenges my clients experience with owning their power is setting boundaries. Usually this is because they are playing a losing game of "shoulds" and "supposed-tos." They feel like they *should* cook a three-course meal each evening instead of getting takeout or asking their spouse to step up and boil pasta once a week. They feel like they're *supposed to* raise their hand for every special project at work to get promoted. Societal expectation is one of the hardest burdens women carry, but it can be one of the most beneficial to drop. Just as we talked about in Chapter 7 on having a growth mindset, changing your vocabulary and then following through with a different set of actions will make a big difference.

What about boundaries in your work-life balance? Working remotely, for instance, can be a blessing and a curse. It's great because we get to be home for the kids or the pets, do the occasional load of laundry between calls, and save on the commute time (and gas money!). However, it can be hard to shut down at the end of the day and decompress before we transition into our household duties. Having a boundary that sets your end time each day is critical to your work-life harmony. In my house, we've always had a "no devices at the dinner table" policy, so we get at least thirty to forty-five minutes per night without any interruptions.

What boundaries are you considering implementing? And why haven't you already implemented them? Is the guilt already bubbling up just thinking about it? Please hear this loud and clear: *having boundaries isn't selfish.* Not even a little bit. Boundaries create a safe and healthy environment for everyone. Consider the rule I have for my kids: no playing in the kitchen when I'm cooking. I didn't set that boundary to be a buzzkill or so that I can live out my Barefoot Contessa dreams. I set it so that I don't turn around with a hot pot of water and scald them as they come running by the stove, or accidently gut them with a knife instead of the fish we're having for dinner.

You deserve to have boundaries, too, so keep in mind that boundaries are only as good as the enforcement of them. If you set a boundary that you aren't going to talk to your friend on the phone every night after work for an hour because it's taking away from the time you need to reach your goals, then you have to actually send her call to voicemail. Otherwise, she'll get the message you're all talk and continue to overstep that boundary.

Setting boundaries can be extra challenging if you consider yourself a perfectionist. You've put such high standards on yourself that you feel the need to constantly prove yourself, which, in the end, makes it hard to prioritize yourself. If you truly want to be the very best you, you're going to have to own your power and set those boundaries. No one else is going to do it for you.

Have the Audacity

While this could easily be coupled with the "Speak Up for Yourself" section we just covered, I wanted to call it out separately because this has been one of my guiding principles since reading *Never Eat Alone* by Keith Ferrazzi. And let me tell you, it has served me well!

What do I mean by audacity? I mean going after what you want with a relentless and bold conviction. I mean speaking up and asking for what you want without any apologies.

What does this look like in practice? For me, it meant calling up my former boss, the president of a large telecom company, and asking him to help me get my book *The Ins and Outs of My Vagina* published. Talk about audacity! But you know what? He did it. He introduced me to his editor, publicist, and agent without hesitation. If I hadn't had the audacity to call him and ask for support, who knows if that book would have had the success it did? Audacity also meant reaching out to Dr. Rebecca Heiss, stress physiologist, professional speaker, and founder of Your Fear(less) Year on Instagram, and asking her for an endorsement of my book. And look how that turned out!

Being audacious allows you to break down barriers and social constraints that we perceive as obstacles so that our wildest dreams can come true. After all, that's what this book is about—grabbing life by the dreams. With a dose of audacity, you'll be sure to go further than you could have without it.

Jacqui's Story

The impact of owning your power can look different for each woman. Here, Jacqui, a member of my Facebook group, Successful Working Women Rocking Reinvention, shares how she found value in this lesson:

> *In January 2022, I felt like I was stuck. I was working in a field that was both emotionally and physically draining. I'd been away from my family for about seven years and felt like I was alone. I reached out to Karin and told her that I was thinking about moving back home to New York. She asked me point blank what was holding me back. In response to what I, at the time, thought were well-reasoned answers, Karin said, "Those all just sound like excuses. If you aren't happy, then why not go for what makes you happy?" I had never heard truer words. I was comfortable but stuck. I was afraid that if I gave up all of those things and returned home, I would be taking a step back.*

> *Soon after our chat, I applied for and was offered a job opportunity that just screamed "Jacqui," working back in New York with teen mothers and their children to help the mothers complete and graduate high school. Though I started slow, within a couple of months the associate director approached me and asked if I would be interested in being the day camp director. He had seen my potential and wanted to "get my feet wet" in leadership. I worked hard and never missed a day.*

Toward the end of the summer, I was asked to be the team's program director, which meant supervising the daycare while holding the case management position that I was originally hired to do.

The entire time that I was making these advancements, I hung on to Karin's teachings, especially "Owning Your Power." I had always known that I was a leader, but I was too shy and too timid to actually go for what I wanted and what I thought I deserved. Because of Karin's lessons, though, I now have more confidence and more knowledge of what I am worth. I am able to harness my power and make a national organization stronger. I have been able to make decisions that have been better for the organization and the clients that I work with daily.

I have taken a program that has been in our area for at least fifty years and made it stronger, even when others thought it would fail. I have learned how to write grants for the program to make sure that it is sustainable. I have taken the role of program director and made this program mine.

I have learned that I am a powerful woman, that I can have the things I want, I can make my own decisions, and I don't have to just blindly accept what's handed to me. I am in one of the best stages of my life. I am living at home with my grandmother who raised me, I am in a position of leadership and making much needed changes for the community, and I am happy. I still have more to learn, but I am in such a different place than I was in January 2022.

So take a page from Jacqui's book: don't wait for permission or validation from others to own your power. (You don't need it!)

You can take small steps every day to assert your power and work toward your goals, whether it's speaking up in a meeting, setting a healthy boundary with your partner or children, negotiating your speaker fee, or pursuing a new business venture. Your dreams hang in the balance, waiting for you to reach out and grab them! You have all the power you need inside of you to make it happen. What are you waiting for?

I hope the answer is "nothing" because when you turn the page, we're going to be diving into Part 3 and the EDIT™ Method, my dedicated system for setting and achieving the goals that will allow you to grab life by the dreams.

Excited? You bet I am! Let's get into it.

• •

Make It Happen

Create a Power Statement

A power statement is a short, positive affirmation that encapsulates your strengths, values, and goals. It can help you connect with your inner strength and remind you of your unique qualities and goals, even in challenging or uncertain situations.

Take the following steps to make your own power statement:

- Start by reflecting on your strengths, values, and goals. Think about what makes you unique and what you want to achieve in your life.

- Write down a list of words and phrases that capture these qualities. For example, you might write down words like "confident," "determined," "creative," "empathetic," or "empowered."

- Use these words and phrases to craft a short, powerful statement that embodies your sense of self and what you want to achieve. For example, your power statement might be something like, "I am a strong and confident woman who is capable of achieving my goals and making a positive impact on the world."

Remember, the power of your statement lies in its personal relevance. Choose words and phrases that deeply resonate with you and evoke a sense of confidence, strength, and empowerment. My power statement when writing this book was, "I am a talented writer with an important message that will change women's lives and have a ripple effect bigger than I can fathom."

Once you have created your power statement, repeat it to yourself regularly, especially in moments when you need to assert yourself or draw on your inner strength. You can write it down and display it somewhere visible, store it in your phone and read it on the go, or repeat it to yourself silently in your mind.

Part 3

EDIT Your Life™

Chapter 11

EDIT™ Methodology

*I'm writing a first draft and reminding
myself that I'm simply shoveling sand into
a box so that later I can build castles.*

—SHANNON HALE

Hey, you rock star you. You just completed Parts 1 and 2 of this book. I hope you'll take a moment to celebrate just how far you've come! It looks to me like you've shoveled a lot of sand into your sandbox and you're now ready to build a castle of your own.

How do we do that?

My methodology.

222 GRAB LIFE BY THE DREAMS

What is a methodology—besides a fancy SAT word—and why am I trying to teach you mine? How will it help you? All valid questions. First, you're probably familiar with a lot more methodologies than you realize. Ever heard of SCRUM, quantitative research, lean or agile processes? Guess what? Yup, those are all methodologies.

I think of a methodology as a series of steps or procedures that can be followed to obtain a proven outcome. I'm sure the *Merriam-Webster Dictionary* has a more studious definition, but at the heart of it, that's what I'm proposing to you. In this case, I'm going to share the exact methods I used to turn my life around and the same process I use with my clients.

Are you excited? I am, too, because I know what's possible when you implement and embody this process.

How the EDIT™ Method Came to Be

EDIT™ is an acronym I came up with when I was building out my first motivational speech. Isn't it amazing how the Universe guides us in that way? There I was, trying to craft a talk that would teach people how to change their lives by sharing my signature process. There was only one tiny problem: I had never articulated my process before! I had lived it, and I had created it, in some ways by happenstance, but I had never even outlined the steps, much less ever taught it to anyone.

As I began brainstorming to make something coherent out of two years of inner work and reinventing myself, I realized my life mirrored the interactions I'd had with my editor during the writing of my first book, *The Ins and Outs of My Vagina: A Penetrating Memoir*.

How could that possibly relate? I'll explain.

While we were revising my book, I would send my editor a chapter for review. He'd read it, then go back through with his red pen and make changes. Some areas of the story would barely be touched, maybe a comma added or removed, whereas other parts would be rearranged, marked up, removed, or altered in some other way. Then he'd send the chapter back for my review. Sometimes I'd accept all his changes, and other times there would be some debate or back-and-forth until we agreed on the outcome. Eventually, the entire chapter would be edited, and everyone would be satisfied with the outcome. We did this for a whopping forty-five chapters, although we only published forty chapters in the finished product. Through all that, not once did he ever send me back a chapter and say, "It's all crap. Ditch it and start over from scratch." Not once. Thankfully.

It was in that realization that the methodology was born. When I work with my life coaching clients, I *never* tell them their life is a mess, that they should throw it all out and start over. Mainly because it isn't! (If you work with someone who says that, it's time to rethink your coach.) Instead, we collectively work to make small tweaks and edits in some areas of life and bigger changes in the areas that need it most. There is always a foundation—areas that are working, which we want to keep as is—and the changes are always made in collaboration. Through deep questioning, challenging thoughts and beliefs, and exploring options for next steps, my clients come up with their own answers, run them through their personal filters, and make the changes that will be most impactful for their lives.

That doesn't mean I don't offer tough love when it's needed or make strong recommendations when they're asked for. I definitely do! It just means the client always has the final say, as do you. It's your life.

Now that you understand where EDIT Your Life™ came from, we can dig into what EDIT™ actually stands for:

E = **E**nvision Your Goal
D = **D**ocument Your Goal
I = **I**nvest in Your Goal
T = **T**ake Action on Your Goal

The subsequent chapters are going to dive into each of these more deeply and expand on what each stage means and how to apply it to your life. You'll also get a series of exercises to help you through each part of the process. It's one thing to read about this methodology and another thing entirely to implement it. I'll hold your hand—virtually—each step of the way.

It can be tempting to read through Part 3 and neglect the application part. At some point, though, you need to stop being a student and start trying new things. You can digest thousands of books, including this one; take millions of free courses; and download a trillion free e-guides, but that will only fill your head with a lot of knowledge, all of it useless if you *do nothing* with it. I know some of you will do your own thing, and as your DIY life coach, I have to respect that. After all, you're in the driver's seat. But I would encourage you to take each section piece by piece and apply it before moving on.

What you have in your hands is a system that works. I've seen it time and time again in my clients. Brenda was able to put her ego in check and overcome her belief that being an art teacher wasn't a good enough career for her when it was exactly what she wanted to be doing in her soul. Celina was able to find balance in her life and prioritize her health in order to avoid a heart attack. Erin even fought through her insecurities and against the naysayers in order to add "TEDx speaker" to her resume, right next to "international best-selling author." Just imagine what you could accomplish!

Before we dive in, here are a few questions you might want to have answered.

Q: Do I have to follow each and every step?

A: Yes. I strongly suggest you do each phase of EDIT™. My personal recommendation is to read each section and immediately engage in the supporting activity. However, if you prefer to get a big-picture view first, you can read each chapter and then come back to the exercises afterward. You might understand how it all fits together better once you understand the full process. You'll also gain an understanding of why each part of the process is necessary. The key is to actually come back and do the work.

Q: Can I do them out of order?

A: I don't advise going drastically out of order. Say you start with Take Action but haven't given the proper thought to the Envision phase. If that's the case, you might be taking a lot of unnecessary or even counterproductive actions, which will cost you precious time and energy. However, there will be times when you are in two or more phases at once. For instance, if you signed up for a course on search engine optimization, that would fall under both Invest in Your Goal, because you're spending money and time learning a necessary skill, and Take Action simultaneously. That's actually a good and totally normal thing. The phases don't have to be worked in complete isolation. If this doesn't totally make sense yet, don't worry. That's what the rest of this section will thoroughly explain.

Q: What if I get stuck? Or fear starts to creep in? Or I get analysis paralysis?

A: I'd be surprised if you didn't experience some level of frustration, confusion, or a sense of being overwhelmed at some point in this process. It's new and it's different, but I've got your back. You can always post questions in the Successful Working Women Rocking Reinvention Facebook group, where you can seek support from me and your fellow members in the community.

Q: How quickly can I complete the EDIT™ process and live my best life?

A: I wish I could give you a simple, accurate number. The reality is, it depends on the size of your goals and the pace with which you take action. Most of my clients have seen some reasonably significant success in four to six months while other clients have taken closer to a year. Think about it: if you want to use this process to improve your work-life balance, you can knock that out pretty quickly. If you want to use this process to write and launch a book, that could take longer. The good news is that takes some pressure off you to have it all figured out in a short period of time.

Q: Is this process "one and done"?

A: It's meant to be a repeatable process you can use for the different seasons of your life. You can both come back and revisit your goals *and* follow the same process as new ones are added to your list. Once you learn the EDIT Method™, it can be applied over and over again. It's the gift that keeps on giving.

I'm sure some of you will have additional questions, but hopefully they will be answered as you go through the rest of this section. You'll probably notice there's no "Make It Happen" section here, but that's because the following four chapters are their own workbook-style sections.

Ready to dig in?

Go ahead! Turn the page! I can't wait to see how you EDIT Your Life™.

Chapter 12

Envision Your Goal

*The only limit to the height of your
achievements is the reach of your dreams and
your willingness to work for them.*

**—MICHELLE OBAMA, SPEECH, 2008
DEMOCRATIC NATIONAL CONVENTION**

I had been stuck in thirty-five minutes of extra traffic on top of
my commute, which was already an hour and fifteen minutes
long, when I burst in the front door of our New Jersey home.
To say my blood was boiling was an understatement. I'd had
the day from hell, which seemed to be an ongoing trend,
defending a $140,000 price tag on the latest trade show my
team was attending.

My second grader came running up to me and shoved a paperback book into my hands. "Look, Mommy! My book is here." His class had put together a book with artwork from each student showcasing what they wanted to be when they grew up. Looking down at his wide eyes and beaming grin, I forced a smile.

"Great, honey. Let me put my things down." I struggled to shake loose from my purse and laptop bag as my dog and other son bombarded me with kisses. I shouted a simple, "Hey," to my husband, who was cooking dinner in the kitchen, no doubt starving due to my late arrival.

"Okay, can you show me your page?" I asked my son, pulling up a chair beside him at the dining room table. "What did you say you wanted to be?"

"I'm going to be a basketball player when I grow up."

Knowing full well it would take a miracle for that to happen, given I'm five-foot-one on a good day and my husband is just under six feet, I encouraged his dream. "That's awesome! I'll come to all your games and cheer you on."

"I'll buy you a car so you can get there," he squealed with excitement.

"Deal." We shook on it to make it official.

He showed me a few more pages his friends had created, then walked away to play with his brother until dinner was ready. I was left alone at the dining room table with my thoughts and a book of childhood dreams. I started flipping through the pages, chuckling or sighing at the ideas. I began to turn the pages more quickly; I was searching for something— some sort of validation that would never come.

"Huh, would you look at that? Not one. Not a single kid," I blurted.

By now my sarcastic tone had caught the attention of husband. "What are you talking about?"

"This book. Not a single kid said they wanted to grow up and be a B2B marketer. That's weird. No one wants to work twenty-four seven and make PowerPoint presentations all day? No one wants to be underpaid and undervalued? No one wants to get reamed out by their boss about a trade show or get told by Sales they suck on a weekly basis? I just find it funny, y'know."

It was anything but funny. It was yet another realization that I had in fact burnt out and stopped dreaming. I had accepted a default life, and it was no one's fault but my own. That, my friends, was the hardest pill of all to swallow.

Remember when you were a kid and you had big dreams for your life? I was going to be a famous dancer married to a New York Giants football player; I was going to live in a mansion. Maybe you were going to be an astronaut or a singer? At one point, I wanted to go to Cornell University and be a lawyer who would argue for the good guys. Maybe you dreamed of getting a full scholarship to Harvard? Later, I dreamed of being a pharmacist and helping sick people feel better. Maybe you wanted to be a veterinarian or a stand-up comedian? Or maybe, like me, you wanted to work as a grocery store cashier so you could scan groceries and push all those glorious buttons on the register. *Click, click, click.* That sounded so satisfying as a child!

What happened to those dreams? Where did they go? Did they get squashed by a teacher, a parent, or a "friend"? Perhaps they faded over time because you realized they weren't a good fit for your desired lifestyle. Or maybe you didn't believe you were good enough, so instead of risking failure, you bailed on your dreams.

There are loads of reasons why our dreams don't come to fruition, but hope is not lost. There is still one way your dreams can come true. How?

You dare to dream big enough.

It all starts with the thought that it's possible for you. That's where the first step of EDIT™ comes into play. It happens when you take the time to envision your goal in its fullest sense. In essence, it happens when you begin to dream again. You dream without the self-editing that your adult brain is accustomed to, without the self-doubt, not to mention the immediate worry about *how* it will happen.

But wait, have you forgotten how to dream?

I can relate. When I was working in corporate, any dreams I had felt dashed and unattainable. I hadn't bothered to dream since I gave up on acting. Fortunately, dreaming is a bit like a muscle. It's something you can practice, restrengthen, and improve.

What does this look like in practicality? How can you uncover those bold ideas hidden deep in the depths of your soul? It starts with trust—trusting you have those dreams in your heart and on your mind for a reason. They were uniquely placed within you, for you and you alone to fulfill. I personally believe no one is given a dream they can't achieve. What a cruel joke that would be, to be given a big vision for your future that, like a carrot on a stick, was moved farther and farther away with every step toward it! Thankfully, it doesn't work like that. (Phew.)

I can't tell you how many clients come to me, going on and on about how they have no idea what they want to do. Suddenly, in the middle or at the tail end of our initial forty-five-minute discovery call, their subconscious will take over, and they'll lay it all out on the table. Here are a few of the dreams my clients have shared:

Secretly, I've always wanted to be a doula.

I've always wanted to write a book, and I know exactly what I'd write about.

I went to school for physical therapy; I should have followed through on it.

I really want to finish my degree.

I started writing a movie script but never finished it.

I'd love to go back to teaching.

It's crazy, but on some deeper level we *all* know what we really want to be doing. We all know our true purpose. We've just done such a good job of burying it that we need to do some digging to unearth it. What's even more interesting is that, before they shared their dreams with me, each one of these women had said they were stuck and had no idea what they wanted to do. Then, each of them went on to articulate exactly what their heart was calling them to do.

Next you can start jotting your dreams down on paper. The reason this listwriting works is because if we just leave our goals floating around in our heads, they're not only unformed, but they're also in there, rattling like loose change among other ruminating thoughts like how much we hate our jobs. In other words, by taking the time to consciously think about your dreams and put them on paper, you're giving them a fighting chance. You're cutting through the noise and heightening your awareness of what your intuition and sub-conscious are telling you.

In addition to moving your goals from your subconscious mind to your active thoughts, you've opened up a safe space to admit to your dreams. A lot of times we keep our dreams buttoned up because we feel people will pooh-pooh them. This isn't a time for judgment, but if you need a little nudge to get in the proper mindset, here's something I like to use with my clients. Imagine your younger self when you think of your dreams and goals. You wouldn't tell your five-year-old self that her dreams were dumb or unattainable, would you? Of course not.

You may need that safe space for yourself because, addi-tionally, most of us are not one-dimensional. We don't want to do just *one* thing with our lives. I have clients who want to volunteer *and* have a day job. I have other clients who want a side hustle *and* to grow in their faith. I have still other clients who want to be more present with family and start a business. There are a multitude of things we are capable of achieving, but when we want it all at one time, that's usually when things get a little crazy. That's around the time that you get overwhelmed and throw your hands in the air, defeated.

And that's where my signature exercise comes in handy. It not only helps you explore various goals, but it helps you organize them in a non-overwhelming way. Ready to get started? Grab a notebook or laptop because it's about to get messy. I personally love paper for this, but do what works for you. An app like Trello or Asana could be a helpful visual.

This is the fun part. You get to tap into your inner child and begin dreaming again!

Envision Your Goal: Doing the Work

Start by outlining your goals under the big categories of life. For example, what are the personal goals you have? The professional goals? The spiritual goals?

Don't self-censor at this point. Like in a brainstorming session, there are no bad ideas here. The usual categories are as follows, but don't be afraid to buck the status quo and come up with a category of your own.

Personal

_____

_____

_____

Professional/Career

_____

_____

_____

Spiritual

_____

_____

_____

Relationships (Friendship / Romance)

_____

_____

_____

Health and Wellness

_____

_____

_____

Finances

_____

_____

_____

Now write out your goals that pertain to each category. For example, my health goals might look like this:

- ☐ Lose fifteen pounds
- ☐ Eat healthier meals
- ☐ Set a good example for my kids
- ☐ Work out three times a week
- ☐ Learn to play tennis
- ☐ Meditate regularly
- ☐ Go on a health retreat
- ☐ Complete a detox

Come up with as many goals as you have and write them all out. Repeat this for every category. I know this is going to seem like a lot, but that's the point. You're rejoining your heart and your head. You're dreaming and brainstorming!

Once you have this initial list written out, go back and revise it, then put your goals in priority order.

Why is revision necessary here? Because we didn't initially self-censor, some items you brainstormed may not actually be goals. For instance, above I suggested, "Set a good example for my kids." Yes, that is something you may want to do, but that's the outcome of your goal, not the goal itself. The goal is to get healthy *so that* you can set a good example for your kids and so that they will be healthy as a result. With this in mind, we'll remove "Set a good example for my kids" from the list, and it will become the *why* that keeps you motivated instead.

My new and revised health goals, set in priority order, are:

❑   Complete a detox/cleanse
❑   Lose fifteen pounds
❑   Eat healthier meals
❑   Work out three times a week
❑   Meditate regularly
❑   Learn to play tennis
❑   Go on a health retreat

From here you should select your top priorities, two or three from each category, and organize them into one final, prioritized list. There is no right or wrong way for this list to be ordered. Take note of what you feel like you "have to" put first. Is that really what you want to be the most important? Where is that feeling coming from? It may take a few tries to get the list down just the way you want it. That's okay and perfectly normal. Your list is a living and breathing instrument. I recommend revisiting it as you accomplish your goals, replacing any one achieved goal with one new priority from your list, and revisiting on a yearly basis as part of your yearly planning.

My first time through, I had thirty-three items I wanted to achieve on my final list. My first mentor and coach, Tamara McCleary, advised me to focus my efforts on my top five goals. I mean, I'm good, but I'm not a magician. There was no way I could do all thirty-three things on my list and do them well. I had to start making some tough but empowering choices.

My final list looked something like this:

❏   Be a more present wife and mom
❏   Get my finances in order so I can make my exit plan from corporate
❏   Write and publish a best-selling book
❏   Start and scale a six-figure coaching business
❏   Be more active in the community and volunteer

See how much more manageable and less stressful that was than a list of thirty-three goals? It was solid guidance that I now pass along to my clients, which is why I advised that you only take the top two or three priorities from each category.

Now, you might be wondering, *What about all the rest of my goals?* Don't worry; they aren't gone for good. They're just on hold for later, after you accomplish your top-priority dreams first.

Once you make the final version of your list, you have a few options for what to do next. Some of my clients like to visually represent their dreams in a vision board. This can be a really effective tool. Plus, they're fun to make and a great reminder of your dreams that you won't be able to ignore. Alternatively, you can display the list in written form on your desk or your refrigerator, wherever you'll be able to see it regularly.

Armed with my final list, I had a new sense of hope and control over my life, something I hadn't felt in a very long time. Everything felt really possible for me, and it will for you too. Even though writing a book was a big task, writing my goal down on paper brought clarity to my foggy mind. I now had in writing the definitive path I wanted to follow without all the other noise that had previously clogged my mind.

Some of you are undoubtedly thinking, *That's it?*

Yep! That's all I had to do to gain clarity. It really is so simple, yet many women never take a pause long enough to complete this step. Some of you have yet to pull out your notebook and make your list. (Yeah, I see you.)

What are you waiting for? Clarity is within your grasp, but you have to do the work.

For my type A personalities, you're probably trying to make your list perfect, to get it right. Well, this might disappoint you, but there really isn't a right or wrong way to do this. Focus instead on what feels good and authentic to you for your life. Let go of the perfectionism. Trust your intuition. It won't steer you wrong.

Now that your big dreams are down on paper, you might be wondering what's next? How do we get them from goals listed on paper to actionable steps? Pop over to the next chapter to take your dream to the next level in the document phase.

Use the space below to work through your big dreams:

Personal

_____

_____

_____

Professional / Career

_____

_____

_____

Spiritual

_____

_____

_____

Relationships (Friendship / Romance)

_____

_____

_____

Health and Wellness

_____

_____

_____

Finances

_____

_____

_____

Other

_____

_____

_____

Chapter 13

Document Your Goal

*Take your dream, start taking action, and before
you know it your dream will be a reality.*

—CATHERINE PULSIFER

Manifesting only gets you so far.

Read that again, my friends. Seriously, I love manifesting as much as the next lady, but at some point, the dream needs to leave your head and become solid steps with tangible actions that will make your dream a reality. I have a feeling this is where a few of you tend to get hung up in the process. You're thinking, *Wait. You mean I have to actually do something*

244 GRAB LIFE BY THE DREAMS

to achieve my dreams? Yes, and most likely that something is going to be *way* out of your comfort zone. So giddyap.

I probably could have chosen a quote about getting out of your comfort zone to kick off this chapter. There are plenty of them floating about, and with good reason: most adults can't stand the feeling of being unsure of themselves or their chances of success. Yet Tony Robbins has said that one of the most basic human needs is a level of uncertainty. In other words, we all need a little spice in our lives. The way to take this leap of uncertainty without fear, but instead with spicy excitement, is to have a plan. Luckily, that is exactly what this step aims to give you!

Once you've envisioned your goal, it's time to document it. In this chapter, you'll learn how to list out the practical steps you'll take to attain your goals and how to organize those steps into a manageable timeline. But first, you're going to take each of those goals and turn them into—you guessed it!—a SMART goal. For a refresher, the "SMART" in SMART goals stands for Specific, Measurable, Action-Based, Realistic, and Timebound. Feel free to revisit Chapter 3 for more information.

Let's imagine you want to open a gym that caters to women. Your SMART goal might be "I want to open a women's gym by August 1 with at least 200 active members in the first six months of operation." Armed with your SMART goal, you can now begin to put the steps into place.

One challenge at this phase is looking at all the things you need to accomplish to realize your dream. I know just how overwhelming it can be. To achieve your gym ownership dreams in the example, you'd likely need to do all the following and more:

- Research franchise options
- Come up with a name for your gym
- Write a business plan
- Register your business
- Research the best equipment
- Purchase a web domain
- Open a business bank account
- Build a website
- Find a location and purchase a building
- Meet with an accountant
- Create job postings
- Interview personal trainers and staff
- Market the business to get customers
- Come up with merchandise to sell
- Host a grand opening party
- And a bunch of other things I haven't thought of but any gym owner will tell you I'm missing

Feeling overwhelmed yet? That looks like a pretty tall mountain to climb. Maybe it's better off left to someone else?

No way! You were given that dream for a reason. Instead of looking at all the items on that list and feeling like you need to do them today or at the same time, documenting your plan can help you spread this list of responsibilities and require-ments out *over* time. Identifying key milestones will help keep you on track without you having to look at everything at once.

For most people that will be a big sigh of relief that makes the goal more tangible and attainable.

When it comes to creating your plan, I recommend you start by choosing a deadline for when you want the goal to be achieved. If I wanted to open this gym, I'd choose a realistic timeline for opening.

How do you determine a realistic timeframe? Talking to a current gym owner, doing a quick Google search, or making a guesstimate are a few ideas. I know a guy who opened a gym in New Jersey, so if I was going to open one of my own in South Carolina, you can bet he'd be the first person I called to review my plan. Since he's in another state, there is no way we'd be competing. (I'd avoid asking a random gym owner in your town, who is less likely to be forthcoming with information.)

The length of time it takes to launch a gym can vary depending on several factors, such as the size of the gym, its location, the availability of funding, and the extent of renovations or construction needed. From what I found online, it can take anywhere from a few months to a year or more to launch a gym. Let's say, based on your research, you feel that twelve months is an achievable timeframe, but you want plenty of room for error, so you tack on six more months to alleviate some pressure. That seems like a realistic goal that is still aggressive enough to keep you moving forward. (Comparatively, if you told me you were going to plan for five years, I'd guess there was some deeper fear holding you back.)

Bottom line? The first thing to remember when making your timeline is to plan for it not to go according to plan, so padding can be helpful for us type A personalities that like to underpromise and overdeliver. Now that that pressure is off, you can relax and enjoy the journey.

Understanding our launch date allows us to break things down over the defined timeframe—in this case, six quarters. You can start by loosely planning out what needs to happen in each quarter.

Why quarters? Daily tracking is too granular at this stage of your goal planning, while yearly is too big a picture. If you truly have a goal that will take five years, then yearly might not be a bad place to start. Meanwhile, if you have a goal that can be achieved in two months, then by all means start with something more detailed, like a weekly plan.

Sample launch plan:

Q1

- Research franchise options
- Choose a name
- Write a business plan
- Meet with accountant

Q2

- Register the business
- Open business bank account
- Research best equipment
- Find a location and purchase a building

Q3

- Purchase a domain
- Build a website

Q4

- Purchase equipment

Q5

- Create job postings
- Interview and train staff

Q6

- Market gym memberships
- Develop merchandise to sell
- Host grand opening party

Geez, this plan looks good. Maybe I should open a gym? I'm kidding, but this hypothetical goal is feeling super attainable already. In fact, I was actually thinking eighteen months may be too long a timeline. What about you? Are you feeling empowered now that we've divvied up the tasks into quarterly activities? I hope so.

Once you have a rough draft of your quarterly plans, it could be a good idea to gutcheck your plan with someone who has been there, done that. You'll notice that in this example, I mentioned creating a business plan in Q1. Most likely the activity we just did would be part of that business plan, and often the local Small Business Administration office has entrepreneurs who can come alongside you and ensure your plan is solid.

Gutchecking doesn't have to be that formal either. If your goal is to get promoted at your company and you've created a plan that you think will help you achieve it, you might want to meet with your boss or another senior advisor to see if they agree.

I know my ladies with control issues are dying to get more granular. As a Virgo myself, I can relate. Not to worry; that's the next step. From here you can take Q1 and break it down into monthly, weekly, and even daily activities. I'd caution against turning the entire first quarter into daily plans, though, as that will only lead to frustration when things get off schedule. Instead, break it down into monthly tasks; then, at the start of each month, take those tasks and break them into weekly tasks. At the start of each week, take your weekly tasks and assign them to a specific day.

Remember that you may need to make adjustments to the plan as you go. That's totally normal. I recommend regular check-ins with yourself, your accountability partner, and/or your coach if you have one. These can be weekly, monthly, or quarterly depending on the person you're checking in with. If you have a goal of quitting smoking, you might need more regular check-ins at first, whereas if you're starting an eco-friendly clothing company, you may only check in with your board of directors annually. Adjusting your plan doesn't mean you're doing something wrong. In fact, if you've ever worked a corporate job, chances are you've had to create a yearly plan for your role or team. Do you recall many years where the plan went exactly as you laid it out? In my fifteen years, I recall zero years that it went perfectly to plan.

Don't put undue pressure on yourself now that you're doing something new. It's hard enough without being your own worst enemy.

Now that the steps to your goal have been documented across a timeline, you can figure out how you want to manage it. You may choose an Excel file or a tool like Asana or Trello, or maybe you like good ol'-fashioned pen and paper. You may want to print your monthly plan out or have it on your desktop screen so you see it each and every day. There is no right or wrong way to do it. Choose what serves you best.

The important thing is you've now got a clear plan to follow to make your dream a reality. If you've come this far, you're light-years ahead of all the people still confining their unique dreams to their heads. Take a moment to celebrate yourself. For real! If you've taken the steps to document your plan, I want you to treat yourself to something special. Maybe it's a fancy dinner out or a new pair of shoes. Maybe you want to get yourself a new yoga mat or take an extra-long coffee break on Friday. If you want to continue being successful, you need to stay motivated, and as I've shared before, celebrating your wins is a great way to do just that.

Kudos on coming this far. There are only two more steps to discuss, and then you'll be well on your way to that dream life you've been desiring.

Document Your Goal: Doing the Work

Use the space below to create your quarterly plan for one of your SMART goals. I've given you space for a two-year goal, but your goal may not take that long to accomplish. Then repeat the process for your other goals:

SMART Goal:

Year 1 Plan

Q1

_____

_____

Q2

_____

_____

Q3

_____

_____

Q4

_____

_____

Key Milestones:

_____

_____

Year 2 Plan

Q1

_____

_____

Q2

_____

_____

Q3:

_____

_____

Q4

_____

_____

Key Milestones:

_____

_____

Chapter 14

Invest in Your Goal

*I will not just live my life. I will not just
spend my life. I will invest my life.*

—HELEN KELLER, *THE OPEN DOOR*

In case you haven't realized it by now, I am not afraid to give you a little tough love. Emphasis on the word *love*. It comes from a place of wanting you to succeed beyond your wildest dreams. The place where your five-year-old self would be in awe of you and your accomplishments.

So here it is: *dreams take investments.* For instance, if someone said they wanted a lavish retirement but hadn't even opened an IRA, would you think their dreams were close to becoming reality? No! You wouldn't think they'd even gotten them off the ground.

Your dreams might not even necessarily require the kind of investment you're thinking of. Typically, we default to money when we hear the word *investment*, but there are several other types of investments we can make toward our goals. Oh sure, if your dream is to own a collection of sports cars, you probably need some money to make that happen. But if your dream is to start a business as a virtual assistant, the barrier to entry is going to be a lot lower and more affordable. My initial consulting business was less than a thousand dollars to start. All I needed to do was register my business for a few hundred dollars, buy a mouse and camera for my laptop, and purchase the Outlook software. (All of which were tax write-offs, by the way.) But even with that financial investment, I still wouldn't have had a profitable business without other critical investments. I had to invest time and energy into getting clients, among other things.

We're going to explore different areas you might invest in to reach your dreams. Once you have a handle on them, there are workbook-style questions in the back of the chapter to help you clarify where specifically you should focus your attention, time, and money. Bottom line: what you invest in and how you invest should always match up with your SMART goal and goal documentation.

When I say invest in your goal, I'm really thinking about investing in a handful of key areas. I call them the TEMPL of Your Dreams: **T**ime, **E**nergy, **M**oney, **P**eople, and **L**earning.

Let's break each of these down further to ensure comprehension and application.

Time

Dreams don't come to fruition if we don't spend time making them happen. This seems like a no-brainer, yet so many people say how little time they have to focus on their dreams.

Now is the time to get serious about how much of your own time you're willing and able to allocate. If I had a dollar for every time someone said they didn't have time to make their dream happen, I'd be a billionaire. How sad! But it's not really a time issue; it's a prioritization and self-sabotaging issue. That is, you either haven't prioritized the actions that will make your dream happen, or you are actively working against yourself, possibly in ways you don't even realize.

Prioritization happens on a daily basis. When you schedule your life around a specific show or sporting event, you are prioritizing that action. When you put your kids and their activities and academics first, you are prioritizing your children. One of my clients came to me for business coaching and shared that she hadn't made a single dollar from her business yet. When I started peeling back the onion, I discovered she had no structure for when she was working on her business, which meant she wasn't sharing her offer enough and inviting people to work with her. She only put time in when the mood struck her, which was rare. In our first session we worked out her new schedule, which consisted of a two-hour focus window each morning from 9 a.m. to

11 a.m. Within her very first focus session she accomplished something she had been dreaming about for five years but had never taken action on: she wrote and launched her first blog post and even posted it on social media. She was overcome with emotion, allowing herself to experience tears of joy for following through on the promise she had made to herself so long ago. That's the power of putting dedicated time toward your goals.

Now it's your turn to prioritize your dream and goals. By the way, this doesn't mean you have no time for anything else. When I started my memoir, I began with only fifteen minutes a day to write. It was all the time I could carve out while raising two young children and managing a stressful full-time job. But slowly I began to find thirty minutes, an hour, and then two hours a day to commit to my manuscript. The more we make time for our dreams, the more time we find for them. Don't let time be a lame excuse.

Just as we need to determine where to spend our time, we need to identify where we *won't* spend our time—at least until our goal is achieved. Maybe serving on the PTA isn't in the cards this year. Maybe coaching your kid's softball team will have to wait. Or maybe you won't worry about getting promoted this year so you can focus on family. There is no right or wrong answer, per se; it's all about priorities and what matters most to you in this moment.

Suze Orman, a notable American financial advisor, advocates for her clients to track their spending so they know where their money is going. Why not do the same for your time? You might even track time versus money (i.e., how much time you have to spend to earn a dollar with one activity versus another). I bet you'll find some areas that could be adjusted. Self-sabotage may look like scrolling aimlessly on TikTok for hours. Odd how you found so much time for that fruitless task when you could have been doing the very things needed to drive your goal over the finish line. (Tough love, remember.) Binge-watching three seasons of your new favorite show in a weekend could have been time better spent.

I'm not saying you shouldn't have a way to decompress or hobbies to indulge in on occasion. What I am saying is that your excuse of not having enough time doesn't hold water.

Maybe you have time, but you're sabotaging yourself out of fear? Time to take action anyway. Do it scared. I did, and look how it's turned out for me.

Energy

You will undoubtedly need to expend some energy to reach your dreams. This includes brain power, pushing through when you feel lazy or tired and tapping into your reservoir of physical and mental power without giving up. Some days, it will be easier to expend your energy than others. On a day where you have a big win or hit a milestone, you'll get a sudden rush of energy fueling you forward. On days where everything seems to go wrong, you may need to dig deeper than ever.

You'll also want a gauge for how you'll measure the things that are worth your energy. I call this ROE, return on energy. What is the impact you're seeing from the energy you're spending in that area? If your goal is having a closer relationship with your kids, it should be pretty clear what is giving you a good ROE, but other goals' ROE can seem almost counterintuitive at times. For instance, posting to an audience of 75,000 on Instagram where no one actually pulls out their wallet and buys anything seems like a pretty low ROE. Alternatively, having a private Facebook group of 1,500 where everyone is engaged and purchases your products seems like a good place to spend your time and energy.

However, you need to be cautious that you're not giving up too quickly or changing your strategy month after month. It takes time and consistency to build your dreams. Just because something seems like it isn't working doesn't mean it isn't. Facts, like easy-to-track key performance indicators (KPIs), can help you separate reality from your feelings. Landing page visits, click-through rates (CTRs), and sales calls were how I first tracked the progress of my budding business. (And hey, if you're not the sort of person who wants to spend the time learning to do this or creating reports each week, then maybe that's a financial investment so you can have these data points!) Meanwhile, if you're trying to quit smoking, the only metric you need is how many cigarettes you smoked that day. A coach or third-party mentor can be very helpful in assessing where your energy might be best spent.

If you're like me, constantly dreaming up new ideas can be an area where you start to overexert yourself. Focus can be your best friend. Come back to your SMART goals and see how your energy is aligned. For example, I started writing a one-woman show for my memoir while I was writing this book. I very quickly reminded myself of my core goals for this moment and put that project on hold. Of course, this will evolve and change over time, so make sure you check your ROE regularly.

Money

No beating around the bush: there will likely be things you need to put some dollars behind in order to achieve your dream.

Be sure to ask yourself, What are the big areas you want to invest in? How will that money help your dream advance? Trust me; there is a lot you *can* spend money on when you're pursuing your goals. The key is to determine what will actually provide a return on investment (ROI). When I first started as my boss's chief of staff, the first thing I invested in was a new wardrobe and a pair of C-suite-approved shoes. Of course, the latter isn't an actual thing, but I had my eye on one brand. I went to the mall and got myself a $650 pair of Salvatore Ferragamos, the black patent leather peep-toes with the bow. #IYKYK. It was my statement that I belonged on the third floor in the executive area and an investment that was well worth it. It gave me the confidence that I belonged, at least in terms of outward appearances. Not every investment is created equal, as my editor Jessica Hatch so rightly pointed out during the creation of this book. As a freelance editor who makes most of her business connections behind a computer screen, the shoes may not make sense to purchase—even if she wants them realllly badly. I couldn't agree more! If she ever decides to become a foot model, I might support the purchase.

It's important to discern when to spend and when you're spending for spending's sake. Pay attention to your thoughts around the purchase. If this sounds like you—"If only I had the right software, then I'd start making money"—you might be using this an excuse for your lack of confidence. Try comparing what the service or product offers with what your goals are. If you aren't purchasing it for any other reason besides investing in your goals (e.g., time pressure, peer pressure), it might not be for you.

Depending on your goals, you may not initially realize all you need to spend money on. Having some sort of budget or cap can be helpful as well. When I was getting ready to launch my first book, I thought all I needed to do was schedule a few social posts to get the word out. *Wrong.* Before I knew it, I found myself in need of a book launch coach to help me navigate all the things that needed to happen to give my self-published book a fighting chance. That was $3,000 of unplanned investment, but I had carved out a marketing budget which I was able to pull from for the expense. And let me tell you, it was worth it.

Additionally, the budget will give you something to hold you accountable and avoid overspending in areas that aren't relevant or needed at the initial stages of your investment in your dreams. For example, when I first started my coaching business, I had a big enough network that I didn't need to worry about SEO. About two years in, I realized I was going to soon tap out my network and could work smarter by hiring an agency to do my SEO and Google Ads.

Money investments come in all shapes and sizes. I spent more than $40,000 writing, producing, and marketing my first book, *The Ins and Outs of My Vagina*. Yikes! But I knew if I didn't invest properly, given the content, it could go south real quick. (Ha, "south"…no pun intended.) It could've ended up in some pretty raunchy territory if I wasn't careful, which is why I was comfortable investing so much money in an editor and cover designer.

Some of you might be thinking: *And that's why I will never write a book. I don't have that kind of money.* Well, I know other authors who have spent less than $3,000 to write, produce, and market their book. Excuse busted. You don't actually need loads of money to bring most of your dreams to fruition.

If you aren't willing to invest a lot of your own money, you can look at using other people's money, or you may need to invest in other areas. For example, you can invest in growing your network, look to angel investors, try a platform like Kickstarter and do crowdfunding, and/or invest more of your own time and energy instead of paying someone else to do the tasks for you.

Some financial investments will be good investments, and some will be poor choices, and the answer will only be revealed through the rearview mirror. (Sorry, type A girlies! I know I'm definitely stressing you out now.) The point is, you make investments based on what you know at the time and adjust as needed over the course of achieving your goal.

Some of you that have a poor relationship with money, you may need to do some work on money mindset before you begin investing financially. Not to worry; I have some helpful resources on my website if this is an area you struggle in.

People

Quite possibly your biggest assets are the people you surround yourself with. They will all fill a different need or function, none necessarily more important than the other. You'll have:

- your champions, people who love what you do and want to share it with everyone they meet;
- your referral partners, if your goal is a professional or entrepreneurial one, who will send you qualified customers for your business's product or service;
- your door openers, movers and shakers who are well-connected and can make vital introductions;
- your mentors, who can show you the ropes because they've been in your shoes;
- your cheerleaders and promoters, whether someone formal like a coach, a sponsor at work, or just friends who are supportive and keep you going;
- and your customers—yes, you already know people who want what you offer.

For those in corporate, you'll also want to identify your bench, people who can backfill you in a promotion situation as well as the talent you'll pull along to build your team. You'll have mentors to guide you and sponsors that can advocate for your advancement. For entrepreneurs, invest in getting to know people who can guide you, can make things happen by opening doors, or will do some work for free. This may involve bartering services or products at the start. The question is, Who do I need in my network to help me get my dream where I envision it going?

Chances are you already have these people in your network; you just need to identify and leverage them. Start by going through the contacts in your phone or LinkedIn connections. Who do you know, and what bucket(s) do they fall into? Having this road map will make your goals more attainable. Conversely, there may be some people you need to "uninvest" in. That may include people who tend to be energy drains (e.g., negative people, people who ratchet up an unhealthy sense of competition in you, maybe even toxically positive people who won't allow you to complain even to the point of sorting through how you're feeling about something important). Sometimes, it may be more benign, such as in the case that a person has played a role in your life for a season, but now the relationship doesn't make sense to continue.

Building relationships is a two-way street. It's always easier to ask for a favor when a favor has been done in return. It can be tempting to take, take, take, but I know from experience, the relationships you nurture and pour yourself into will bear the most fruit. Offer yourself selflessly to other people's success, and they will reciprocate.

Once you have mapped out the people you want to invest in, you need the audacity to reach out to them, as I mentioned in Chapter 10. It's so important that it bears repeating. A list of people is only as valuable as what you do with that list. Remember when I tapped into my network when I was interviewing for a job in the energy sector? I have no doubt that made a big difference in me being offered the role. Besides, what good is a network if you can't ask for support when you need it?

Are you ready to boldly ask for help? I hope so. It's a game-changer.

Learning

You'll surely need some combination of your time, money, and energy dedicated to learning new skills to up-level your capabilities and bring your dreams about, and that's normal. Identifying the skills most critical for you to learn will be helpful at the Investment stage. And you'll need to start considering what you can do on your own and what you will outsource. For example, if you're leading a department and have responsibility for its profit-and-loss reports, you can't outsource your financial acumen. You'll need to take a course or acquire this knowledge from a mentor. There is also value in learning to do some of these things on your own so you have domain knowledge and can speak the language.

Some learning can be acquired quickly, like a one-hour course on how to grow your Instagram following. Other learning will takes weeks, months, even years, like which products you should scale and invest in for your business and which to cut or modify.

Other things will be better off outsourced. I have no desire to learn how to use WordPress, the platform that my website is designed on. I now pay a developer to manage this for me, and it's worth every single penny. What things do you absolutely need to learn, and what could you offload?

Fight the temptation to become a permanent student. I see my clients tempted to spend many of their early days as an entrepreneur taking every free training course they can get their hands on. They assume someone else has the silver bullet that will suddenly make their business pop. Their thirst for knowledge becomes a crutch, crippling them to the point they aren't taking any of the right actions. They're busy building email funnels and learning how to use Instagram when all they needed was to be out talking to people and focusing their efforts on connecting with ideal clients.

Don't be overwhelmed by how much there still may be to do. That won't serve you. Instead, feel empowered that you have a road map to ensure your success and begin to enjoy the journey. If you outline which areas above you want or need to invest in at each of the documented phases of your plan, you will be well on your way to success.

I just got chills typing that. It's that powerful. Investing in your goal encompasses a lot of factors, but once all of your investing and divesting is under control, it's time to move on to the final step: Taking Action.

Invest in Your Goal: Doing the Work.

Use the space below to more closely consider your investments in the TEMPL areas of your goals.

Time:

Where am I spending my time daily?

_____

_____

_____

What distractions or time-sucking activities can I get rid of to prioritize my goals?

_____

_____

_____

At what time of day am I most productive/do I have the most energy for my dreams?

_____

_____

_____

How can I ensure I have more time in those windows to work on my dreams?

_____

_____

_____

Energy:

Where do I enjoy spending my energy?

_____

_____

_____

Does that answer align with my goals? Why or why not?

_____

_____

_____

What drains my energy?

_____

_____

_____

How can I do less of that? What do I need to say no to?

_____

_____

_____

Money:

How much money do I think I'll need to bring my dream to life?

_____

_____

_____

How much money do I currently have to spend on my dream?

_____

_____

_____

In what area(s) would that money be best spent?

_____

_____

_____

What priority level would I assign to each of these items? 0 = lowest priority; 10 = highest priority

_____

_____

_____

If I needed more money, where might I get it from? Would that money come with interest or expectations in return?

_____

_____

_____

People:

Who in my network can support my dreams? How?

_____

_____

_____

Who is missing from my network that I need to add? How will they help me?

_____

_____

_____

Who can I help in return and how?

_____

_____

_____

Who in my network do I need to distance myself from? Who is not supportive of my dreams?

_____

_____

_____

Learning

What skills or knowledge do I absolutely need to advance my goals?

_____

_____

_____

What skills can I pay someone else to do? What specialized knowledge can I pay for?

_____

_____

_____

What skills or knowledge do I want in the long run but can get by without in the short term?

_____

_____

_____

Chapter 15

Take Action

There is only one proof of ability—action.
—MARIE VON EBNER-ESCHENBACH

My first vision board, back when I had first heard about *The Secret* on *Oprah*, is the perfect place to start this chapter, as it offers an important lesson about taking action. Since I didn't have any poster board at the time, I used a black corkboard I had up for important messages in our apartment. I stripped it bare before I eagerly began tacking the images of my new vision up. I was in a hurry to finish before my boyfriend got home. I wanted to surprise him with our new life!

The keys jingled as he let himself in. My moment had arrived. I ran to the front hallway to greet him, board in hand.

"Sit down, sit down. I gotta show you something," I panted.

"Can I get a drink first?"

"No. This is important. It's gonna change our life."

Realizing I meant business, he slid his sneakers off and found his way to the green couch we'd purchased from Bob's Discount Furniture. I stood on the opposite side of the coffee table and propped the board up for him to see.

"There's this thing called *The Secret*; I saw it on *Oprah*." I qualified my source so he knew it was legit. "Basically, if you think it, it will happen. So I put all the things we want to get on this board. That way, the Universe will know what to give us."

He sat completely motionless, tolerating my exuberance.

"So look, you know I want a ring at some point, so that's on there. And we'll want some kids, probably two, but I think you can update it and add more and take them off if you change your mind. And I'd love a sports car. I'd be fine with a BMW, but why not go for the biggest and best first? So I chose a Lamborghini. And what's really going to change everything is the lotto ticket. We're gonna win the lottery."

Still he sat there quietly, although it seemed as if a gear had started to shift in his mind.

I myself shifted nervously. *Maybe I overwhelmed him with the wedding ring?*

"Karin...."

"Yeah? Why aren't you more excited? This stuff works! One woman put a picture of a stove on her vision board, and she got it."

"I have a question for you."

"What?" I couldn't understand what he could possibly be questioning.

"Do you play the lottery?"

"Well, no, not right now. But maybe. I guess I might."

"Seriously, Karin. You have to play the lotto to win the lotto. And I know you. You aren't going to spend any of your hard-earned money on lotto tickets."

I burst out laughing, but it was more of a nervous laugh. He was right. There was no way in hell I was going to put up the kind of money you need to statistically win the lotto. I reached over and took the tack out of the lotto ticket image and placed it in the trash.

My boyfriend patted me on the head as he walked by to the kitchen. "Don't worry, you might still get that ring."

Whoa—wait. I did a double take. "Might?"

That was my first vision board but certainly not my last. Fortunately, I've gotten better and more methodical with each one. Unlike my first attempt, I now understand that a well-designed and focused vision board is only one piece of the puzzle. You can envision your dream all day long, have positive thoughts, and document solid plans on paper, but if you never take any action and invest in your goal, it's all just a fun crafting project.

Some of you may be wondering if there is a difference between investing in your goal and taking action. While they can sometimes be one and the same, I'd like to offer up a very clear distinction. Taking action is intentionally moving the ball forward in a meaningful and productive way. Some women will use being busy and taking action for the sake of action as a way to convince themselves they are investing in their goal. For example, rather than launching your website with the bare minimum, you might fuss over color, fonts, and other design facets. Those "actions" feel like you're making progress, but you're really avoiding the biggest and most important action: launching the website and selling your service or product. Ideally, Taking Action is the sum of the first three steps in the EDIT™ Method all being enacted. If you've done your due diligence during the Document phase, you should be taking the proper actions, but if you're unclear about how your actions support your goal, it's likely best to have a coach or someone you trust to guide you through it.

Are you still on the fence about taking action? Think about it this way: Do you want to look back at your life in five years and say, "I wonder what would have happened if I'd....."? Or do you want to look back and say, "I'm so glad I followed my dreams"? Whatever your answer, you're the only person holding yourself back. It's now or never.

With that said, I know that sometimes we need a little help; an extra push, if you will. Accountability is one of the biggest missing ingredients for most women when it comes to reaching your goals—especially when it comes to taking new actions. Especially if they are uncomfortable actions. By holding yourself accountable, you're more likely to stay motivated and keep yourself on track. Many times, this can be achieved with simple measures, such as adding tasks to your calendar, having a daily to-do list, tracking your progress, or celebrating your wins.

Without accountability you have no real, immediate consequences for not achieving your goal, which means there isn't much extrinsic motivation right away to stick to your goals. Of course, the consequences *are* real and will *eventually* be realized, usually materializing as regret. If you require something deeper to keep yourself going or you aren't prepared to hold yourself accountable, my next two tips should do the trick.

Staying True to Your "Why"

One way you can hold yourself accountable is to go back to your Why. What is your unique purpose? Why are you pursuing this dream in the first place? What legacy do you want to leave? If it's a strong enough Why, you should be able to motivate yourself into taking the right actions.

At some point your dream becomes bigger than you. Bigger than your fears and insecurities. Bigger than the rejection or uncertainty you might face. It becomes about the greater good—the person you were destined to become so you could have the impact on others you were born to have.

Just reading this far in my book is a big step in the right direction. Look at you taking action without even realizing it. Way to go!

Using an Accountability Buddy for Full Steam Ahead

How can you stay accountable if you're worried about self-regulating or have a tendency to flake on yourself? Get an accountability partner.

An accountability partner offers you several benefits. They provide you with emotional support and encouragement when you need it the most, they offer constructive feedback, and they give you the extra push you need to stay on track.

Where do you find an accountability partner? It could be a spouse, friend, coworker, church member, life coach, or other person in your life. There is no limit to who it could be as long as that person has your best interests in mind. The key is to find someone who is willing to check in with you regularly and keep you on track. It's why people who have a workout buddy or someone to walk with them are more likely to get in their daily exercise. If one of you doesn't feel like going, the other can push you to get up and do it. The same goes for getting a new job, starting a business, or whatever else you want to do. You can ask the person supporting you what goals you can support them on in turn. This way you'll have a reciprocal relationship, although that certainly isn't required.

Working with an accountability partner can take some getting used to. It can be helpful to share up front what you respond well to and what might turn you off. I have some clients that love a direct push and others that respond to a gentle nudge. Some love motivational or inspirational messages to keep them on track while others recoil from that approach. The more up-front you can be about your expectations to your accountability partner, the more smoothly things will go.

Similarly, not everyone makes a good accountability partner. If you have a friend who's always skipping her workouts to go for margaritas after work, she's probably not the best pick for a workout accountability partner. On the other hand, if part of your dream life is having more fun and rekindling your passions, she may be the perfect accountability partner to get you out and about. Thankfully there's no rule that says you can't change your accountability partner, so you can always switch things up if it's not working.

When it comes to accountability partners, you have a person not just giving you advice or answers to your burning questions but actively investing their own energy into seeing your dreams succeed! In a way, accountability partnership is how your dream goes from internalized to externalized, out in the world, something other people than you are aware of.

As a coach, it's my job to hold my clients accountable for their actions. One of the ways I do that is through my private Facebook group: Successful Working Women Rocking Reinvention. If you haven't joined yet, that's a great action to take now. Another way I hold my clients accountable is through text, email, and the app Voxer. Sometimes I send them messages to make sure they're working out when they said they would or to check in on how their journaling is coming along. Sometimes I'm holding them accountable for doing the inner work and other times for taking bold actions. The point is, they aren't going through it alone, and you shouldn't have to either.

So there you have it, my four-step EDIT Methodology™:

E = **E**nvision Your Goal
D = **D**ocument Your Goal
I = **I**nvest in Your Goal
T = **T**ake Action on Your Goal

It's not complicated or rocket science. It's simple, straightforward, and, well, it just works! When you put in the effort and follow through, anything is possible. I wouldn't have written a book if I didn't think you could do it. (Yes, *you*.) I would have just kept coaching people privately. But I knew this book had the opportunity to change so many people's lives, including yours and from there all the lives you'll impact. I just couldn't risk keeping it that close to the vest.

Now is *your* time to Grab Life by the Dreams. Ready to put it all together and see the final outcome? Keep going; you're about to Rock Your Reinvention.

Take Action: Doing the Work

Use the space below to consider your Why and map out your accountability plan.

My Why:

_____

_____

Is it the same for each SMART goal, or does it vary? If it varies, how so?

_____

_____

Accountability Plan:

Who will help me stay accountable?

_____

_____

What style of support do I require from them? What would be most helpful for me?

_____

_____

Besides having an accountability partner, how else can I hold myself accountable?

_____

_____

EPILOGUE:
ROCK YOUR
REINVENTION

*We all have a reinvention inside us, waiting to get out. All
we have to do is give ourselves permission and go for it.*

—KARIN FREELAND

Back in Chapter 1, I said the jury was out on whether I could
live my dream life or not. Well, not only am I living it, I am
happy to say that I feel truly worthy to live it, and I'm loving
every moment of it! Every time someone leaves a five-star
review for one of my books, every time a client graduates
from my program, every time I earn money for my services,
and every time I get to be present with my husband and kids,
I know deep down in my soul I'm living my purpose and
having an impact on the world. I know I've rocked my reinvention. And the rocking doesn't stop here—as life goes on
and seasons change, I will continue to reinvent myself when
and where it's needed.

By now you've learned how to control your inner critic
and step into your newly created confidence. While there's no

silver bullet to reinvent your life, I know if you put all of the steps and tools we've covered in this book into play, you'll get there. Getting unstuck and discovering your purpose is a journey to be enjoyed, not to be hurried through as if the end state is all that matters. If you savor each step along the way, you'll be sure to pick up on more signs from the Universe and to be more in tune with your own truth.

As you've seen from a handful of client examples, I'm not the only one who has changed her life for the better. I've had the privilege of interviewing many women on my show, *Rock Your Reinvention*, all of whom have reinvented some aspect of their lives. Every time I speak to a woman who has undergone this change, instead of comparing myself to her, I'm inspired to keep going and growing because her achievements are proof that we all have it in us to succeed. With the right mindset, we all have the power to create a new destiny, write a new chapter of our lives, and own our power. Why shouldn't you be able to do the same? There's absolutely no reason that this process won't work for you too.

Below I'm sharing a few final stories about my clients' reinventions, told in their own words, so you can learn from their experiences, avoid their pitfalls, and be inspired to take action on your own goals. (Be sure to head off any temptations of comparison as you read their stories. This is meant to motivate you and give you new perspectives to relate to!)

Kate, on setting boundaries and owning her power:

Prior to working with Karin, I was rotting in a dead-end job that was not using my talents, appreciating my capabilities, or showing any opportunities for the future. I knew I needed to make a change and that the worry, anxiety, and self-doubt I was experiencing were preventing me from taking a step forward. I needed to know what I wanted next; I needed to rediscover my mojo before exploring my next career move.

The first quick win was getting back into an exercise routine. Investing in my own self-care reminded me that I was strong, capable, and deserving. It helped recharge my energy and let me tap into forgotten passions. I also worked on boundaries (i.e., locking the bathroom door to keep my kids out) to make sure I had my space.

With Karin I worked on boundaries, confidence, and figuring out what I wanted most in life. I discovered that what I desired more than anything was to be a mom—a fun mom! It brought light to my priorities and how I was going to invest in those areas by hosting barbecues and creating fun mom moments.

As a result of the way coaching gave me time to truly focus on what I wanted and needed, the Universe started listening and showing up with the right opportunities. I turned off work at a reasonable hour and stayed in the moment with my family, leading to a greater sense of happiness and calm.

Since coaching I have been in situations at work where I've received soul-crushing feedback that for the first time in my life I didn't take personally. It burned, pissed me off, and made my cry, but I realized that the feedback was not about who I am or how capable I am. I now recognize it was one person's perception of the situation and a missed opportunity by a fellow employee who wasn't managing their own stress well to provide constructive feedback.

Since coaching I have not backed down from hard conversations, and I have realized that my purpose in life is growing people, both those at work and, more importantly, my little people at home. I am designed to have hard conversations and to make things, people, and processes better.

My advice to other women who want to reinvent their lives is to get help, ensure you have someone holding you accountable for the changes you commit to, always believe in yourself, and, then, when you're ready, take a leap.

Erin, on reframing her mindset and cutting out negative self-talk:

At the beginning of my coaching relationship with Karin, I was only scratching the surface of what was going on. There were many messages I kept hearing from my past as I tried to work on my top three goals, ones that were holding me back. Karin and I dug deep into those messages, and the act of reworking them into positive thoughts helped to change my mindset. We were then able to jump in and start putting together a plan, first to work on my overall confidence and second to achieve my goals. My goals that I started with shifted as we worked on defining them and clarifying my passion and purpose.

Karin provided me with empowering exercises and perspectives that have helped enhance my productivity and optimize the time I spend working toward my goals and purpose. We discovered I was saying yes to everything, which meant some of my activities were not aligned with my passions at all. Karin helped me remove these activities from my list of priorities in order to open up space for what was aligned. The more I opened up, the more impact we were able to make on regaining control of my life. My fear of failure and of judgment have been enormous in the past, but I have taken giant leaps to stay focused on myself and not let those fears derail me.

My advice to those who are reading this is to always show up no matter what—do not let fear stand in your way. The right opportunity is out there for you. Stay consistent, be authentic, and believe in yourself. Be present in each moment, enjoy each day to the fullest, and make sure what you are doing brings you joy.

Celina, on building unshakable confidence and turning inward:

Do you ever feel unworthy? Perplexed about what others see in you? I did too!

Early in 2021 I was working a job I thoroughly enjoyed, for the best leaders I've ever had the honor of following. They gave me the title of vice president, with the business cards and responsibilities to match. To say I was humbled is an understatement. I couldn't understand what they saw in me to justify that title. I struggled to introduce myself as a VP to new acquaintances, especially since I knew I had some work to do in areas like being more strategic and communicating more effectively. I told myself I should be humble about this big title, and so, like a little mouse, I went on quietly doing my work to the very best of my ability. I couldn't imagine expressing my feelings of unworthiness to others.

Enter Karin, which marked the beginning of the biggest transformation I've ever experienced.

Breakthrough #1: I am worthy of this and more!

Working with Karin, I was able to identify the root causes of my feelings of unworthiness. I had found a safe space to discover, share, and work through what was fueling my negative self-talk. Honestly, I didn't even know I was doing it! Significant wins from our first year working together include improved communication, strategic thinking, and beginning to discover who I really am. At forty-four years old, this was a long overdue exercise. Karin's interview series, *Rock Your Reinvention*, and the Success without Sacrifice group program helped me to refocus on areas of my life that I'd been neglecting, like my relationship with my husband.

Breakthrough #2: It is okay to love myself!

For a long time, I'd identified as a servant leader. Even in my personal life, I lead a life of service to others, and I love that. It makes me happy. Somewhere along the way, though, most likely very early on, I started believing that others should always come first, long before me.

The meetings with the ladies of Success without Sacrifice were life-changing. In this space I felt safe to share my feelings and was able to see that putting me (more specifically my health) first was not selfish.

When we worked on our goals, my 30-60-90 plan was health- and "me"-focused for the first time in my life. When most of us hear "self-care" and "self-love," we think of a mani-pedi or a facial or a massage session. While it can be good to do those things, first, I needed to tackle some tougher challenges, like smoking cessation and realizing I was at very serious risk of a heart attack, which required immediate changes to my diet and exercise regimen. My VP title would be irrelevant if I wasn't around to own it. Can you say that working with a coach saved your life? I can! And for that I am grateful!

Breakthrough #3: I am confident!

I'm now able to set healthy boundaries at work and at home. I took my first work-free vacation in eight years and have since unplugged numerous other times. By refocusing on my core values, removing distractors, and delegating, I've built a foundation to anchor myself to. With refocused value on myself and my health, I can keep working on living a better, more fulfilled life.

My advice to other women is to build a support network around yourself. Having a sisterhood or group of allies helps you keep going and realize you aren't alone. You are worthy of prioritizing yourself. You never know—it just might save your life.

Mary Beth, on listening out for messages from the Universe to find her bigger purpose:

I was caught in a cycle of negative self-talk (mostly questioning my abilities), with a sense of disconnect from my values and the type of culture I wanted to work in. I thought the business I worked for wanted to create real change in our corporate culture, but this came to feel like an empty promise when, time after time, I was ignored, even as I was caught up in the middle of unnecessary turmoil. It created a fear of being put down, of not wanting to "say the wrong thing," and of my ideas remaining unheard.

I have a strong faith and thought if I kept praying that my fears and concerns would be resolved. I felt guilty for not being strong enough to overcome them. My breaking point was when I started to feel fatigue and stress, which resulted in sleepless nights and an overwhelming feeling that I wasn't good enough to fix this situation. I knew I wanted to make a change, and I needed help to sort through it.

This is why I'm so glad I reached out to Karin. Immediately, I got clarity on my "why" and my goals, which included finding a new job. She pushed me to go beyond my surface-level goals and dig deeper to understand that work doesn't define who I am. Once I got my goals down on paper and was honest with myself, the idea of achieving them became less scary. I started to have fewer sleepless nights and felt like I was in control.

In the past, I have been very hard on myself and have always strived to achieve more and do, do, do. Through coaching, my mindset has been modified to think through why I'm pushing myself and to question if I can modify my expectations and still achieve the result I want. Maybe I don't need to vacuum the house today; maybe it can wait until Friday before company visits. Learning to control my inner critic has been one of the biggest benefits I've experienced in my life reinvention.

Now, I work for an amazing company where I have a better work-life balance. Even though it's an ongoing challenge for me not to take on more projects or work, I have more confidence in speaking up and enforcing my boundaries. I'm also listening more, not only in work relationships, but at home too.

My advice is: don't let fear of the unknown hold you back. Always allow yourself time to recharge. If you can change your thinking or how you respond to situations, and if you can take breaks, you'll feel more in control and actually be able to give more of yourself in every aspect of your life.

Brenda, on rekindling your passions:

After taking some time off work to raise my children, I began interviewing for jobs in my field, as a creative producer of visual content within publishing and media. Time and again, I would get to the end of the interview process, and it would be me versus someone else. For one reason or another I wasn't landing the gig. After I got a no from my dream job, I decided to take a pause from interviewing.

It was a new year, and I thought maybe I wasn't on the right path. I felt defeated. I had also recently lost my mother, which made it difficult to focus on my work-related issues. I was ready to get back to a full-time career, but I wasn't 100 percent sure I was loving my old one. I wasn't sure what to expect with reaching out for career advice, but I knew this was the time to make changes.

Education was something I had always thought about, but I had some hesitations about embarking on this journey at forty years old. Karin asked me to start journaling about my reservations, and once I gave myself permission to be honest and not judge what I was thinking or writing, I knew what I was destined to be: an art educator. I applied to graduate school, got in, and started working toward a second master's degree. I was hired that summer to teach at a private school, where I could gain more experience while I worked toward my certification. I now know it's never too late to change or move into another field. It is beneficial to take time to find your authentic self at each stage in your life.

I'm also starting to enjoy writing again and creating art by allowing time for myself. Carving out time to journal and find the right path for the current me versus the younger version of me has been so helpful. It has been liberating to really have something for myself.

Visualization and other mindful writing and meditative prompts have guided me to design a clear career path. I am rediscovering parts of my old self that existed before I had children. I have always been ambitious, but now my priorities are different, and I am accepting that. I feel at peace about my decisions. Although grad school feels challenging at times, I work through those difficult moments. Karin's guidance has been helpful on numerous occasions when it all feels like too much. The mindful work we do before each session I go back to time and again to center and ground myself.

My advice to readers is that you have the answers; you just have to listen. Also, sadly, nothing comes easy. There are times I'm still anxious about things pertaining to my career, but I am thankful for the new tools I have to help me work through and process these anxieties. I am happier because I know I am on the right path for me, and I know you will be too.

You can join the likes of these amazing women who refused to settle for status quo. You, too, can run headlong into reinvention. Regardless of your age, status, experience level, financial situation, or background, you have the power to revamp your life.

Now, it's officially your turn to rock your reinvention. You have all the tips and techniques to do it.

...but do you have the guts? Are you excited to learn what life looks like on the other side of reinvention? The intrinsic motivation to make the necessary changes? Do you want it badly enough? Those are the questions you get to answer for yourself.

If you screamed yes, then you're *beyond* ready to Grab Life by the Dreams—you're ready to live it!

ABOUT THE AUTHOR

Karin Freeland is an author, speaker, certified life reinvention coach, and entrepreneur. Her mission is to help corporate women get unstuck, discover their true purpose, and live a life they absolutely love. Her first book, *The Ins and Outs of My Vagina*, was released in September 2021. It debuted as a number one new release in Amazon's Sex and Sexuality category before going on to receive several accolades, including a Readers' Favorite gold medal and three BookFest Book Awards.

Karin is an alumna of the State University of New York Brockport, where she earned two bachelor's of science degrees in dance and business. After fifteen years in corporate America, she broke out to become a full-time author and entrepreneur.

Karin grew up in Upstate New York, but now lives in Greenville, South Carolina, with her husband, their two boys, and their dog, Kobe. She enjoys yoga, ballroom dancing, gardening, and outdoor activities.

Learn more about how Karin transforms women's lives at www.karinfreeland.com/life-coaching. You can connect with Karin on Instagram @karinfreeland and on Facebook at https://facebook.com/KarinFreelandLifeCoaching.

SOURCES

Introduction

Reuell, Peter. "Lessons in Learning." *Harvard Gazette*, September 4, 2019. https://news.harvard.edu/gazette/story/2019/09/study-shows-that-students-learn-more-when-taking-part-in-classrooms-that-employ-active-learning-strategies/.

Chapter 1

Chowdhury, Madhuleena Roy. "The Neuroscience of Gratitude and Effects on the Brain." *Positive Psychology*, April 9, 2019. https://positivepsychology.com/neuroscience-of-gratitude/.

Chapter 3

Doran, George T. "There's a S.M.A.R.T. Way to Write Management's Goals and Objectives." *Management Review* 70, no. 11 (1981): 35–36. https://community.mis.temple.edu/mis0855002fall2015/files/2015/10/S.M.A.R.T-Way-Management-Review.pdf.

Matthews, Gail. 2007. "The Impact of Commitment, Accountability, and Written Goals on Goal Achievement." Paper presented at Dominican University of California Psychology | Faculty Presentations, San Rafael, CA. https://scholar.dominican.edu/psychology-faculty-conference-presentations/3

Hebb, Donald O. *The Organization of Behavior*. New York: Wiley & Sons, 1949.

Chapter 5

Irving, Zachary C., Catherine McGrath, Lauren Flynn, Aaron Glasser, and Caitlin Mills. "The Shower Effect: Mind Wandering Facilitates Creative Incubation During Moderately Engaging Activities." *Psychology of Aesthetics, Creativity, and the Arts.* Advance online publication. 2022. https://doi.org/10.1037/aca0000516.

Tomioka, Kimiko, Norio Kurumatani, and Hiroshi Hosoi. "Relationship of Having Hobbies and a Purpose in Life With Mortality, Activities of Daily Living, and Instrumental Activities of Daily Living Among Community-Dwelling Elderly Adults." *Journal of Epidemiology* 26, no. 7 (July 2016): 361–370. https://doi.org/10.2188/jea.JE20150153.

Xia, Ning, and Huige Li. "Loneliness, Social Isolation, and Cardiovascular Health." *Antioxidants & Redox Signaling* 28, no. 9 (March 2018): 837–851. https://doi.org/10.1089/ars.2017.7312.

Chapter 6

Editors. "Why Did So Many Christians Support Slavery?" *Christianity Today*, 33 (1992). www.christianitytoday.com/history/issues/issue-33/why-christians-supported-slavery.html.

Marshall, Joey. "Are Religious People Happier, Healthier? Our New Global Study Explores This Question." Pew Research Center, January 31, 2019. www.pewresearch.org/short-reads/2019/01/31/are-religious-people-happier-healthier-our-new-global-study-explores-this-question/.

Chapter 8

"Are Extroverts More Confident? (A Complete Guide.)" PsychReel, October 6, 2022. https://psychreel.com/are-extroverts-more-confident/.

"Cognitive Triangle: How Are Thoughts, Feelings, and Actions Connected?" PsychReel, September 22, 2022. https://psychreel.com/cognitive-triangle/.

Lechter, Sharon. *Think and Grow Rich for Women: Using Your Power to Create Success and Significance.* New York: Penguin, 2014.

Chapter 9

Sneed, Rodlescia S., and Sheldon Cohen. "A Prospective Study of Volunteerism and Hypertension Risk in Older Adults." *Psychology and Aging 28*, no. 2 (2013): 578–586. https://doi.org/ 10.1037/a0032718.

Team Tony. "Discover the 6 Human Needs." Tony Robbins.com, 2023. www.tonyrobbins.com/mind-meaning/do-you-need-to-feel-significant/.

"Volunteering May Be Good for Body and Mind." Harvard Health Blog archives, December 31, 1969. www.health.harvard.edu/blog/volunteering-may-be-good-for-body-and-mind-201306266428.

Milton Keynes UK
Ingram Content Group UK Ltd.
UKHW020942280923
429557UK00013B/469